THE LIFE
OF
BLESSED ELIZABETH CANORI MORA
MOTHER & MYSTIC

Translated from the Italian,
with a Preface
By

LADY MARY ELIZABETH HERBERT

MEDIATRIX PRESS

MMXVIII

ISBN: 978-1-953746-28-3

Blessed Elizabeth Canori Mora: Mother & Mystic

This edition is reproduced from *The Life of the Venerable Elisabeth Canori Mora,* originally published in 1878 by Burnes and Oates and now in the public domain. The typesetting and layout of the present volume ©Mediatrix Press 2018, and it may not be reproduced for commercial purposes or provided as a whole in physical or electronic format without permission.

Mediatrix Press
607 E. 6th Ave.
Ste. 230
Post Falls, ID 83854
www.mediatrixpress.com

TABLE OF CONTENTS

Protest of the Editors of the "Annales De La Sainteté" of the Nineteenth Century............................... ix

Preface to the English Translation........................ xi

Preface of the Author................................ xiii

CHAPTER I
    Birth of Elizabeth Canori.—Names given her in Baptism. —Her amiable character in childhood.—She is confided to the Religious of S. Euphemia, and afterwards to those of the Monastery of Cascia.—Returned to her family, she by degrees loses her fervour.—Finding it impossible to become a Religious, she resolves to contract Marriage.—Gloomy prognostics regarding the Future.... 1

CHAPTER II
    The Venerable Mother is exposed to the perils of vanity and worldly pleasures; is preserved from them by a salutary affliction.—Our Lord miraculously saves her life.—Infidelity of Christopher Mora.—Two pious relatives go to reside with Elizabeth; they console her in her trials.—She leaves the Vespignani Palace, and goes to live with her father-in-law.—She displays heroic virtues in this new position.—She gives birth to her youngest child.—Suffering from a mortal malady, she miraculously recovers her health.—Through this new trial, she becomes more holy and more united to God...................... 9

CHAPTER III
    Elizabeth entirely changes her life and becomes quite docile to Divine Grace.—Her new style of Life brings about fresh persecution: Help accorded her by Our Lord and the Blessed Virgin.—Wonderful fruits which she draws from two Retreats.—Our Lord sends her a Director according to her own heart, the Rev. Father Ferdinand of S. Louis..15

CHAPTER IV
    The Venerable Mother proposed as a model to Mothers.—She commences the education of her two Daughters from their earliest years.—She gives them a taste for reading holy books and teaches them

to meditate on Eternal Truths.—She takes pains to form them to the virtue of patience under contradictions and sufferings.—Her eagerness in making them frequent the Sacraments early.—One of her Daughters decides on embracing a Religious Life, the other makes choice of the married state.
.... 21

CHAPTER V

Elizabeth a model for unhappy wives.—Simultaneous deaths of her two sisters-in-law, with whom she had lived on the most affectionate terms.—She sells all that she is possessed of, to satisfy her husband's creditors.—Miraculous cure of her father-in-law.—Christopher Mora is confined in the Convent of SS. John and Paul.—He attempts the life of Elizabeth.—Cruel persecution of Elizabeth by her sisters-in-law in consequence of her husband's conduct.. 31

CHAPTER VI

Death of the father-in-law of our Venerable Mother.—Elizabeth is expelled from the house of the Moras.—She miraculously saves her husband's life.—Extreme affliction caused by her own daughters.—Our Lord assists her in her poverty.—Wonderful history of a picture of Jesus of Nazareth... 41

CHAPTER VII

Our Lord cures a sick person by the mediation of the Venerable Mother.—John Sala provides for the wants of the house, and is regarded as the father of the family.—Miraculous cure of Mary Anne Mora.—Elizabeth receives the gift of miracles.—History of several striking miracles.—Extract from the proceedings concerning the cure of Pius IX.. 49

CHAPTER VIII

The Venerable Mother is chosen to atone for the sins committed in her time, and to appease the anger of Heaven by her sufferings.—The devil is now permitted to make martyrs, and to take the place of tyrants and executioners.—Our Lord, in His goodness, forewarns His servants before they are given up to the temptations of Satan.—The Venerable Mother is prepared by symbolical visions for the battle against Hell.57

CHAPTER IX
Elizabeth is given up to the vexations and cruelties of Satan, to appease the Divine Justice ready to chastise the world.—Unheard-of martyrdom which she endures during nine days and nine nights from the demons.—His Holiness Pius VII. delivers her.—She miraculously recovers her sight and her health.—The Blessed Virgin places the Infant Jesus in her arms.. 63

CHAPTER X
Elizabeth takes the habit of the Third Order of Bare-footed Trinitarians.—Our Heavenly Father threatens the Church with great afflictions.—The Venerable Mother offers herself as a victim of expiation.—Our Lord strengthens and arms her again for the fight.—She submits to a varied and cruel martyrdom.—She is overwhelmed with extraordinary favours in recompense for her generosity.—She drives away the devils by extraordinary means, and obtains a decisive triumph over them.. 71

CHAPTER XI
Our Lord renews His promise to Elizabeth, which He had previously made, of protecting Rome and the Sovereign Pontiff. —Conspiracy against His Holiness Pius VII.—Elizabeth discovers to him in a miraculous manner the perfidy of his counsellors, and he decides to remain in Rome.—She goes to give thanks to Our Lord in the Church of S. John Lateran.—Our Lord gives her a magnificent reception on her return from her pilgrimage.—Ingratitude of the Roman people for so many graces received.. 83

CHAPTER XII
Our Lord prepares the Venerable Mother for interior trials by symbolical visions.—She sees her soul under the form of a sick sheep, and afterwards under that of a pilgrim.—The way of perfection is represented to her by various steep and tortuous paths.—S. Joseph comes to her aid.—Our Lord reassures her, and promises her final perseverance.. 91

CHAPTER XIII
Picture of the various symbolical visions which announced to Elizabeth the graces, gifts, and particular privileges with which Our Lord desired to surround her.—She contracts a celestial marriage with the Spirit of Love.—Our Lord plunges her into the bosom of inaccessible light.—S. Michael introduces her into glory.—She is chosen as the Spouse of the

King of Glory.—She is confirmed in grace.—August ceremony of the mystical marriage.—She receives the glorious insignia of Queen for all eternity.—Wound of love; crucifixion and mystical death.—The Venerable Mother in a state of almost constant ecstasy.......... 99

CHAPTER XIV

Detailed recital of various apparitions made to the Venerable Mother.—Apparition of the Infant Jesus, of Jesus in the Cenacle, of Jesus suffering.—Apparition of the Blessed Virgin under different forms and in many of her mysteries.—Devotional practices by which Elizabeth prepared herself for the Feasts of the Blessed Mother.—S. Peter and S. Paul appear to her in a symbolical vision which relates to our times.—Apparition of a great number of other Saints....... 111

CHAPTER XV

Efficacy of the prayers of the Venerable Mother in obtaining all kinds of graces.—She converts various sinners on the way to damnation.—Miraculous cure of His Holiness Pius VII.—The gift of tears granted to Elizabeth; holy use which she makes of them.—She penetrates the secret of consciences.—Narrative of a young man on the subject of a sin recently committed.—She foretells the future of many persons.—She goes, by the gift of bilocation, to the aid of many different people.................................... 123

CHAPTER XVI

The Venerable Mother is privileged to deliver a great many souls from Purgatory.—Our Lord gives His servant the keys of Purgatory.—She delivers from Purgatory the members of her family, and particularly Cardinal Scotti.—She goes into Purgatory on the Feast of All Saints, and frees a great many suffering souls.—Glorious triumph which she obtains in their favour in the year of her death.. 133

CHAPTER XVII

Our Lord shows, by symbolical visions, to the Venerable Mother the care which He lavishes upon her soul.—Her ardent desire for perfection, and the graces which she obtains.—She makes the Religious vows, and rigorously observes them.—Rule of Life.—She practises it with great perfection.—Elizabeth makes a vow to do what seems to be most perfect. Severity of her penance.—Our Lord draws up for her a more austere Rule of Life.............................. 139

CHAPTER XVIII
>The three theological virtues are the necessary foundation of sanctity.—All the Saints necessarily possessed these virtues in a heroic degree.—Wonderful operations of Divine Grace in creating Faith, Hope, and Charity in the Venerable Mother.—Her ardent charity towards her neighbour.. 149

CHAPTER XIX
>Elizabeth esteems herself as the greatest sinner in the world.—She gives herself up to the lowest and meanest occupations.—Her exercises to obtain holy humility.—Her repugnance to exposing the lights which possessed her.—Terms of deep disdain in which she addressed herself.—Her happiness when she is despised or injured.—Praises were a punishment to her.—Example of her humility in the apparition of His Holiness Pius VI.. 159

CHAPTER XX
>The Venerable Mother, filled with virtue, approaches her end.—Wonderful visions which announce her deliverance, and make her long for Heaven.—Her illness declares itself at the end of 1824.—Its strange and supernatural character.—She is suddenly cured, and when it was believed that she was restored to perfect health, she foretold her imminent death.—Our Lord leaves her the choice of life or death; she prefers death.—She prepares herself for Eternity.—She suddenly expires whilst speaking to, and blessing, her children.— Her burial... . . 167

CHAPTER XXI
>Apparitions and miracles which took place after the glorious death of the servant of God.—She recommends her daughters to her sister, Signora Maria Canori.—She gives advice to various persons.—The sick were instantaneously cured by touching her holy remains, and others by invoking her after her burial.—Various apparitions in the Monastery of the Philippine Nuns dei Monti.—Striking conversion of Christopher Mora, the husband of the Venerable Mother.. 177

EPILOGUE. 187

EDITOR'S NOTE ON THE SUBSEQUENT BEATIFICATION OF
>ELIZABETH CANORI MORA. 191

PROTEST OF THE EDITORS OF THE
"ANNALES DE LA SAINTETÉ" OF THE
NINETEENTH CENTURY

THE titles of Saint and Blessed, which are often used in the pages of *Les Annales de la Sainteté*, are only the expression of our esteem and veneration for the servants of God whose biography we are writing. According to the prescriptions of the Sacred Congregation of Rites in these matters, we have no intention of anticipating the definitive Judgment of the Holy and Apostolic See in their regard. We declare that as regards the wonderful circumstances here related, and not yet approved and sanctioned by the authority of the Sacred Congregation of Rites and of His Holiness the Sovereign Pontiff, our pious readers must give only a purely human credence with respect to the value and authenticity of the documents and the witnesses who are brought forward to guarantee and support their truth.
Respectful and submissive sons of Holy Church, we desire always and in all things to conform ourselves to the prescriptions published by the authority of Pope Urban VIII, especially in the years 1625, 1631, and 1634.

PREFACE TO THE ENGLISH TRANSLATION

IT has been often remarked that in this nineteenth century there are very few Saints, save in the Cloister, among the upper classes of society. Our Lord seems to reveal Himself to the lowly and humble: to the poor seamstress of S. Pallais, to a little goatherd at Lourdes, to the simplest peasants in out-of-the-way and unknown places: while the rich and mighty He "sends empty away."

Yet, now and then, there are exceptions; and one of these is to be found in the biography of the Venerable woman, the events of whose life we are about to give in an English dress to our readers. Her story is full of encouragement and comfort to wives and mothers of every class, but especially to the highest, in these days when domestic happiness (which formerly was the pride and boast of English people) has become so lamentably rare, when the sanctity of the marriage-bond is less and less regarded, and when men and women make no secret of vices which formerly they had at least the grace to be ashamed of and to conceal.

And this melancholy state of things reacts upon the children. There is every day less and less respect for parental authority: less and less natural affection, or consideration for the feelings of mothers, or the duties of sons and daughters. The smallest attempt at authority is looked upon as a grievance, to be resented and evaded. Warnings are disregarded. Self-indulgence and luxury are carried to a pitch which involves an expenditure utterly beyond moderate means. And so the downhill course is rapid: and ruin and misery and dishonoured homes are the result.

And in this lamentable state of things what is a Christian wife and mother to do?

To pray, to suffer, to atone, to bear silently what she cannot help. Never to weary or grow faint at repeated disappointments, at the continual bruising and rending of her heart's best affections. To hope on, to hope ever, to persevere in spite of all, in patience, in charity, in sweetness.

This was Elizabeth Canori's plan: and in the end the victory was hers. Not in a day, nor in a month, nor in a year; not in her own lifetime, even, did she see the fulfilment of her prayers. But after her death all that she had wished for was granted; all that she had suffered bore fruit. And long before that event Our Lord had deigned to make up to her by astounding graces and gifts and revelations of Himself for the mortifications, and sorrows, and privations of her daily life.

So let each of us take heart by her example. Long as our trials may seem to last, yet, viewed in the light of eternity, the most weary life is but as a shadow which cometh and is gone.

Accepting our crosses, whatever they may be, embracing our Crucifix even when its sharp points drive the pain home, let us persevere bravely, bowing under that Divine Will which has apportioned to each of us that which will most contribute to our eternal weal; and so redeeming not only our own souls but the souls of those for whom we have given, maybe, a lifetime of suffering and prayer.

MARY ELIZABETH HERBERT

Herbert House, Belgrave Square,
September 21, 1878.

PREFACE OF THE AUTHOR

THERE ARE A CERTAIN NUMBER OF PERSONS IN THE WORLD ON WHOM EVERYTHING SEEMS TO SMILE: WOMEN WHOSE HUSBANDS HOLD THE HIGHEST APPOINTMENTS IN THE STATE; mothers who may with confidence look forward to the most brilliant future for their children. They are in the full enjoyment of health and beauty, blessed with all the advantages of fortune and position—in a word, nothing seems wanting to their happiness.

But experience teaches us that nothing, in reality, can be more deceitful than outward appearances. The writer of this life once knew a lady of high rank, to whom, in this way, no blessing seemed wanting: every one considered her as the happiest woman in the world. One day this lady paid him a visit, and he could not help saying to her: "Madam, if perfect happiness were attainable in this world, no one would dream of disputing your title to its possession." She changed countenance, and after a momentary pause, replied: "*No one* can judge from appearances. Listen to the secret trouble under the weight of which I am sinking, and you will soon be convinced that I am the most unhappy woman in existence. I have come to seek a little consolation and advice from you as a Priest of God, so that I may not be altogether overwhelmed by the weight of my misery."

We see, then, that even among the small number of those who appear in a truly enviable position, there are some who are suffering a real martyrdom, which is hidden altogether from the eyes of the world. The shelter of home and the privacy of domestic life frequently conceal the most poignant sorrows. Wives are specially called upon to suffer in secret. Mothers have peculiar trials, not only in the education of their children, and in their establishment in the world, but from their frequent ingratitude and misconduct after all the care and anxiety which have been lavished upon them from their birth. Sometimes poverty or reverses of fortune come to add their weight to the troubles which so sadly oppress them; and the heaviest burden invariably falls on the wife and mother.

The subject of this biography, Elizabeth Canori Mora, had more than the usual share of such trials and sufferings. But her earnest faith and piety triumphed over them all; and by her heroic patience and charity she ensured the salvation of all who were dear to her, and arrived at an eminent degree of sanctity. No trouble or disgrace was spared her: the idolised bride became a neglected and ill-used wife; rich and independent, she was reduced to poverty and a condition little better than that of a servant; from being highly esteemed she was despised and contemned by all; and up to the last hour of her life her husband was her greatest cross. But by the aid of Divine Grace and her own correspondence with it, every trial and sorrow was turned into profit for her soul. Even her husband was converted after her death, and became a holy Priest and Confessor.

Her life, therefore, is one full of hope and consolation to wives and mothers, no matter how heavy their trials may be. They will learn from Elizabeth's example that in religion alone can be found the panacea for all evils; that Divine Grace transforms the cross and makes it bear the most precious fruits. So that those things which, humanly speaking, would prove sources of unmixed sorrow, become to the faithful soul fresh elements of sanctification.

There never was a time when it was more needful to proclaim openly these great truths to the world, and force men to see that Christianity alone can enable them to bear up against the many trials of this mortal state.

We learn, too, from Elizabeth's biography that no circumstances or position in life need hinder our sanctification; for she put in practice the evangelical counsels, and attained to a heroic pitch of sanctity under difficulties which would have appeared insurmountable to a less courageous or generous soul. She seems to have been raised up in this nineteenth century to strengthen and encourage all who are fainting under the weight of innumerable burdens; and to kindle in all hearts a more lively faith and charity towards God and the truest fidelity to the Holy See.

There is one peculiarity in her life which deserves also to be placed in a clear light. God allowed her as a child to make a vow of virginity, and then to forget it and embrace the marriage state; and yet, in order to show that His mercy can surmount every obstacle, He was pleased to permit her in the end to receive the "aureole" of Virgins, so that she might "follow the Lamb wheresoever He goeth." This great privilege was likewise granted to S. Mary Magdalene, S. Margaret of Corbona, and several other Saints in the like manner, and was looked upon by Elizabeth as the most signal favour Our Lord had bestowed upon her. Another consolation is afforded to us by this wonderful life; and that is, the evidence hereby given us that the Saints of this nineteenth century are in no way inferior to those in the more glorious eras of the Church.

This Venerable servant of God was adorned with gifts, graces, and privileges equal to any recorded in the Lives of the Saints, and displayed in as eminent a degree the great goodness and mercy of God. She had the gift of bilocation; she was directly inspired by the Holy Spirit to impart information to eminent personages in matters of immense gravity; she helped to avert terrible dangers and tribulations from the Church; she had prophetic visions of a superior order, under the veil of mysterious symbols; and, towards the end of her life, her path was literally strewed with miracles.

She died in 1825; but there are still many persons yet living who knew her, and Rome is filled with the perfume of her virtues. The Cause of her Canonisation is going on well; the ordinary Process at Rome and Marino being ended, the Sacred Congregation of Rites, in its sitting of the 7th of February, 1874, decided that the Cause of Beatification and Canonisation might be introduced, after the permission of His Holiness had been obtained. The late Holy Father, Pius IX., having examined the report of the Secretary of the said Congregation, ratified and confirmed the decision, and with his own hand signed the permission for the introduction of her

Cause; and by the same act, on the 26th of February, 1874, he decreed to this great servant of God the title of Venerable.

The Postulator of the Cause of the Venerable Mother, Brother Antonino (belonging to the Institute of the Brothers of the Christian Schools in Rome), has kindly sent us all the documents necessary to compile this life, together with a *résumé* of the ordinary Process, published under the eyes and with the approbation of the Sacred Congregation of Rites. All the circumstances we have related, therefore, have the testimony of judicial witnesses, and are thus invested with the authenticity which is required in the biography of a Saint.

We have also had the pleasure of holding several conversations with the daughter of the Venerable Mother, Mother Mary Josephine, now Superioress of the Oblate Nuns of S. Philip Neri in Rome. She has been good enough to place at our disposal a very complete memoir of the home life of her holy mother. For twenty-five years she was her constant companion and confidential secretary; and was, therefore, able to supply us with many little details of immense interest.

The nephew of the Venerable Elizabeth Canori Mora, Brother Romualdo Canori, Vicar-General of the Brothers of the Christian Schools, has also expressed his approval of this work. Before commencing it, the author knelt at the tomb of this great servant of God, begging that she might bless these humble pages, so that they might prove a source of consolation and salvation to many sad and stricken souls, especially among wives and mothers; and he feels confident that this petition will be heard and answered.

THE LIFE OF BLESSED ELIZABETH CANORI MORA

CHAPTER I

Birth of Elizabeth Canori.—Names given her in Baptism. —Her amiable character in childhood.—She is confided to the Religious of S. Euphemia, and afterwards to those of the Monastery of Cascia.—Returned to her family, she by degrees loses her fervour.—Finding it impossible to become a Religious, she resolves to contract Marriage.—Gloomy prognostics regarding the Future.

"ROME was the country of my venerable mother," said Mother Mary Josephine; "her father was Thomas Canori and her mother Theresa Primoli, both of Roman origin, and belonging to respectable families, in good circumstances." She came into the world on the Feast of the Presentation in the Temple, 21st November, 1774, and it would almost seem that the Blessed Virgin, who showered so many graces upon this privileged soul, had obtained for her the favour of having her birthday on one of her own great Feasts. The next day her parents presented her at the baptismal font, and gave her the names of Mary Elizabeth Cecilia Gertrude. We shall see from the following narrative in what a high degree of perfection the venerable servant of God reproduced the virtues of her illustrious patronesses.

In her earliest childhood Divine Grace took possession of her soul. As soon as she was able to speak she astonished every one around her by the maturity of her reason and her precocious piety. Whilst yet a lisping child she was truly eloquent when she spoke of the things of God. She listened with the most remarkable attention to all that was said to her on religious subjects, faithfully remembering everything, and when asked to repeat what she had learnt she answered with surprising accuracy.

As soon as her pious parents saw that she was capable of learning, they placed her with the religious of S. Euphemia, who excelled in the difficult task of training children. The Superioress of the monastery, M. Gertrude Riggoli, very soon discovered the wonderful gifts with which Our Lord had endowed the heart of her pupil, and conceived such great affection for her that she desired to have her always near her. At first the child was only a half-boarder, returning every evening to her father's house; but Mother Riggoli desiring to have Elizabeth constantly with her, asked her mother as a favour to allow her to remain at the convent during the night. We believe that the pious child made her first Communion in this monastery, but there is no authentic document in existence to prove this fact. She received the Sacrament of Confirmation in the great Basilica of S. Peter, at Rome, on the 5th July, 1782, and Mother Gertrude Riggoli was her godmother. Up to this time everything had smiled upon this holy child, and it seemed as if Our Lord had desired to shower upon her virtuous family all heavenly blessings and all worldly prosperity. But this state of things was not of long duration, and the cross soon came to mark these fervent Christians with the sign of the friends of God. The sons of Thomas Canori, being grown up, requested their father to make over to them their share of the capital, so that they might go into business for themselves. But they paid dearly for their inexperience, and in a short time they lost all their money and reduced their whole family to actual poverty.

In consequence of the straits to which he was reduced, Thomas Canori was obliged to withdraw his little girl from the Monastery of S. Euphemia, and thus interrupt the education which had so lately been begun. This unexpected change of fortune and condition overwhelmed him, and filled his heart with bitterness. Elizabeth was yet only a child in years, but her mind, formed by Divine Grace, had already taught her to consider all events as coming from God's Hand.

She strove, by loving ways and words, to induce her father to support his trials in a Christian manner, and to adore the designs of a God always just and good, whether He send us blessings or misfortunes. By degrees he began to understand the secrets of the Divine intention, and raising his hands and eyes to heaven, exclaimed with holy Job: "O Lord, Thou hast given me these blessings, and now Thou hast taken them away; may thy Holy Name be for ever blessed!"

No sooner had her father thus humbled himself under the

Chapter I

severely loving hand of God, than the mission of his child was accomplished, and she could return to the solitude of the cloister, there to learn to know God better, and to escape the seductions of a flattering world.

A wealthy relative of Thomas Canori's, sympathising with the painful position in which the imprudence of his sons had placed him, resolved to help him by undertaking the education of his two young daughters, Elizabeth and Benedetta. Thomas thanked God for this unexpected mercy, and conducted them himself to the Convent of Cascia, in order to entrust them to the care of the Augustinian Nuns. This separation was deeply felt by both the father and mother of Elizabeth; it seemed to them that all their troubles were renewed by the absence of the angelic child who had so greatly comforted them. But they generously sacrificed their affection for her to the higher considerations which made this sacrifice a duty.

The entrance of the young girl into the Monastery of Cascia was the signal for her to redouble her fervour; and from this time she made surprising progress in virtue. She explained in the following manner to her spiritual father the wonderful effects which Divine Grace then produced in her soul. "At the age of eleven," she said, "I was received into the Monastery of Cascia, and remained there two years and eight months. My entrance into this cloister was a special favour of Divine Mercy to withdraw me from the vanities of the world which had already begun to take root in my heart. Once within this sacred enclosure, I gave myself entirely to God, by continual prayer, the practice of penance, exercises of piety, and above all, by fidelity to interior recollection, which was increased by solitude and mortification of the senses.

"Very often Our Lord loaded me with favours, sometimes during Holy Communion, sometimes during prayer. At the age of twelve Our Lord one morning ordered me to consecrate myself to Him by a vow of virginity; I immediately obeyed, but without informing my Confessor. At this time I had no director; only Jesus crucified; with Him I arranged my penances, as well as all the rest of my conduct."

The devil, furious at seeing such goodness in so young a child, raised against her one of his perfidious plots, from which a soul could only escape by the aid of heroic patience and abnegation. She herself states that she was accused of "an abominable action," without specifying its nature; and her Confessor himself believed that she was guilty. This cruel trial, far from troubling her, filled her with joy; it seemed to her that God truly loved her, because He gave her a share in His shame and reproaches. On seeing every one turn against her, she became more recollected in God, and arrived at a degree of union with Him which delighted the religious of the monastery. Satan trembled with rage when he saw that his snares against this pious child had only turned to the advantage of her soul; and he resolved to use his efforts to throw her back into the world, where he hoped to find more abundant means to tempt and conquer her; so he made use of her own sister Benedetta to accomplish his guilty purpose. Benedetta cherished in her heart a strong wish to become a Nun in the Convent of S. Clare of Montefalco; but she did not know what measures to take so as to leave the Monastery of Cascia and pass on to the other. However, one day she conceived the idea of writing to her father that Elizabeth was ailing, and that the air of Cascia was not healthy for her. She imagined that on the receipt of her letter, her father, alarmed, would remove both of them, and she hoped that after leaving, she would find means to enter the Monastery of Montefalco. Everything took place as she had foreseen. Thomas Canori, on hearing of his daughter's delicate state of health, was frightened, and went without delay to withdraw her from the convent and bring her home.

The atmosphere of the world must be truly pestilential, when even such virtue as that of Elizabeth cannot resist its influence.

By the care of her family her health was soon entirely restored; but alas! the vigour of her soul was weakened in the same measure as her bodily strength increased. She fell by degrees into a state of tepidity, which had the most deplorable consequences. That strong attraction for the religious life which she had cherished from her infancy was lost, and she forgot that sacred vow of virginity which she had so joyfully offered to Jesus crucified. In proportion as her union with Our Lord diminished, a want of recollection made itself felt, and Elizabeth's mind became more and more distracted. Worldly pleasures, from which she had hitherto lived estranged, began to appear to her under a more agreeable aspect. From the time that she ceased to keep so strict a watch over her senses, more especially that of sight, a door was opened by which the devil could enter into her soul, and work untold mischief. However, her conduct was always, to all outward appearance, innocent and pure; this relaxation of which we speak was entirely interior, and no one would have known anything of it if she herself, in her home, had not spoken of it subsequently to her two daughters.

Even on this subject however, Madame Mary Josephine did not hesitate to say: "I have no doubt that my Venerable Mother thus spoke of her pretended tepidity, in order to satisfy her yearning for humility."

But Our Lord watched over His servant, and all the schemes of the enemy could not defeat His merciful solicitude. Later on, Elizabeth, reflecting on this perilous epoch of her life, when her piety had suffered such an eclipse, could not conceive how she had been stopped on the brink of the abyss, or how she had had the happiness to preserve the purity of her soul in the midst of a corrupt world, to which she had imprudently given herself up with the simplicity of her character, and with all the enjoyment of her age. Whilst she was filled with these thoughts Our Lord appeared to her, and said: "My child, I have seated Myself at the door of your heart, so as to defend it from the entrance of evil passions. I have commanded My angels to shed over your soul a precious liquor, which has the effect of communicating to you a supernatural simplicity to preserve you from evil and to render you inaccessible to the corruption of others." On hearing this consoling revelation, Elizabeth felt her heart inflamed with such love for the Author of so great a blessing, that she could not cease from praising and thanking Him. One of the means used by Our Lord to detach her from the world, and preserve her guileless soul from all evil, was the state of poverty and distress to which her family were still reduced. Their home had become a very purgatory since luxury and comfort had vanished from it; for her brothers, who had been the cause of all these trials and losses, were those who showed the greatest irritation and impatience under their misfortunes.

They could not bring themselves to bear the idea of remaining in an inferior position, after having enjoyed the pleasures which riches can so easily procure; and exerted themselves in every way in hopes of regaining what they had lost. They tried various fresh speculations, always confident of success, and tormented their father to allow them to take from him the small income which still remained at his disposal, and to risk it in a fresh venture. Thomas Canori and his loving wife were cruelly tried by these unreasonable demands, and were consequently in a state of great anxiety and trouble. Elizabeth deeply felt for her parents, and their distress filled her with constant grief. This state of cruel anxiety and suspense lasted for six whole years. Misfortune often brings with it a salutary grace to a well-disposed soul. The desolation and bitterness with which Elizabeth's loving heart was filled, reminded her of the tranquil and happy days which she had passed in the Monastery of Cascia, and the idea of entering religion again presented itself to her mind. "Oh!" she exclaimed, "how contented should I be if I could return to the monastery, if it were only to be a lay-sister!" At such times she would take her Breviary, and retiring into a corner, there pass whole hours reading the prayers and reciting the Psalms. Her sister Benedetta, perceiving the attraction which was reawakening in Elizabeth for the religious life, imagined that she could make use of her to accomplish the wish which she had so long cherished—of consecrating herself entirely to God. She persuaded her to join her in trying to gain admission, both together, into the same convent. Elizabeth

Chapter I

willingly entered into a plan, the realisation of which had become the sweetest dream of her life. They presented themselves together to the Oblate Ladies of S. Philip Neri, in the square Dei Monti, in Rome. But Our Lord, Who had particular views regarding Elizabeth, permitted that these ladies should accept Benedetta and refuse her sister. Benedetta entered this monastery and remained there for many years, till at length she died, leaving behind her so many recollections of piety, that her memory is still revered in the convent. Repulsed from the cloister, Elizabeth fell into her former desolation of heart; no monastery would open its door to her, and to her great regret, she bade adieu to the religious life.

But she was more resolved than ever to leave her home so as to escape from the intolerable trials which daily beset her. There was no way of accomplishing this except by settling herself in the world, and she determined in consequence to marry. Her intention was scarcely known, when several young men hastened to ask for her hand. At this time she had again partially opened her heart to vanity, and she desired to appear with certain advantages in her new position. But for this purpose it was necessary that her husband should have money; and as none of those who offered themselves were men of fortune, she dismissed them one after the other.

In the end her desire was gratified. The son of Dr. François Mora, heir to a considerable property, came to ask her of her parents. Elizabeth danced for joy, and was only happy when she knew that her marriage was definitively arranged. The marriage was solemnised on the 10th January, 1796, she being then twenty-one years of age. Now it seemed to her that she was leaving for ever a state of poverty and trial, to enter into a new world which offered her only pleasure and happiness. Alas! she was far from suspecting that, on the contrary, she was placing her foot on the way of Calvary, and that the Cross which she then embraced, under such promising auspices, would be in other ways more heavy than that which she was about to leave. But if her simplicity and innocence permitted her to be thus deceived by external appearances, maternal instinct had a presentiment of the truth. In the midst of the splendid marriage feast, where everything breathed joy and happiness, her mother, secretly praying, felt her heart struck with a sudden sadness, and seized by a melancholy presentiment, exclaimed: "Alas! I feel my child will not be happy."

CHAPTER II

The Venerable Mother is exposed to the perils of vanity and worldly pleasures; is preserved from them by a salutary affliction.—Our Lord miraculously saves her life.—Infidelity of Christopher Mora.—Two pious relatives go to reside with Elizabeth; they console her in her trials.—She leaves the Vespignani Palace, and goes to live with her father-in-law.—She displays heroic virtues in this new position.—She gives birth to her youngest child.—Suffering from a mortal malady, she miraculously recovers her health.—Through this new trial, she becomes more holy and more united to God.

ELIZABETH left her paternal home to reside in the superb Vespignani Palace. Her eyes were dazzled by the sight of the rich and sumptuous apartments prepared for her; she found there everything which modern luxury could imagine, and believed she had really discovered true happiness, and gained possession of a sort of terrestrial paradise. Her heart began to lay itself open to the attractions of pleasure and vanity. A strong wish for display and to shine in worldly society had taken possession of Elizabeth's mind; and the liberty she enjoyed as mistress of so beautiful a house filled her with delight. But Our Lord disposed all things so well that she soon became more solitary than ever.

Christopher Mora conceived a most unfounded and extraordinary jealousy of his beautiful young wife, and being excessively suspicious, he watched all her movements and her most trifling actions to try and discover some ground for his conduct. Woe to Elizabeth if she cast an innocent look, if she addressed a civil word, or if she smiled upon any man but her husband he became furious, and as he was not easily pacified, the young wife was utterly disconcerted by a conduct as unreasonable as it was unexpected. In order to preserve peace in their home, she determined to live in complete retirement, far from all relations, and out of sight of every one. She restricted her visits to her own family. Her father's house, which she had before been only able to endure by patience and daily victories over herself, became now her only refuge. She breathed more freely in the society of her affectionate and virtuous mother, and of her venerable and beloved father. But she was at last deprived of even this refuge. Christopher Mora became alarmed by her conduct, and was urged on by his passion to forbid her speaking to her own parents. Elizabeth adored the rigorous designs of Heaven, and submitted unresistingly to this unreasonable order. The retired life which she was obliged to lead was most beneficial to her. Being now unable to seek any consolation abroad, she turned herself to God, gave herself up to meditation and prayer, and gradually recovered some portion of her former fervour and peace.

Our Lord, pleased with her docility in corresponding with Divine Grace, desired to give her a sensible sign of His protection, and to show her how precious her life was to Him. One day Christopher Mora amused himself by playing with a pistol in her presence. Elizabeth, knowing it was loaded, begged her husband to fire it off, so as to avoid any accident. He obeyed, but afterwards continuing his game, he directed the weapon towards his young wife, and pretended to fire so as to amuse himself with her fright. At this moment a mysterious voice said to him, "Stop! stop!" and at the same time an invisible hand violently turned the direction of the shot; the ball struck against a picture representing Our Lord upon the Cross, and broke the glass in a thousand pieces, leaving the image intact. The pistol was loaded with two balls unknown to Christopher. He remained paralysed with fear; but Elizabeth understood all that was meant by this extraordinary preservation, and resolved to give more entirely to God the life which He had so miraculously saved. Afterwards, she never could think of this occurrence without shedding tears of tenderness and gratitude.

During these alternations of joy and sorrow, the young wife had the happiness to become a mother. The birth of this first son so gratified Christopher Mora, that he entirely forgot his jealousy. He troubled himself no more regarding the conduct of his virtuous wife, and gave her full liberty to go where she pleased. Again Elizabeth cherished the illusion that she should at last enjoy happiness. But such was not the design of God. Our Lord had chosen her to be a living holocaust, and desired to have her constantly near Him on the Altar of the Cross.

Her husband's feelings changed by degrees from exaggerated affection to profound disgust; he even attached himself to a person of low condition, whose conduct was infamous, and gave himself up to this shameful passion with such madness that to gratify it he did not fear to despoil his own family, and expose his wife and children to all the sufferings of poverty.

This time the chalice which the Divine Hand presented to Elizabeth was filled with a double bitterness. Deserted and unhappy wives alone are capable of appreciating all the intensity and humiliation of this new sorrow. After a time, however, it would seem that Our Lord found that this Cross was too heavy for her, and prepared an unexpected alleviation to her sufferings. Christopher Mora had two pious and virtuous sisters, who had scarcely become acquainted with Elizabeth than they conceived the most tender affection for her. Her example inflamed their piety, the sweetness of her words enchanted them, and the experience of her wisdom made them desire to have her as a guide in the way of perfection. They begged their parents to let them come and live in the house of their sister-in-law, and their great wish for this arrangement obtained for them the desired permission.

Two companions of such rare piety formed a sweet and agreeable society for Elizabeth; and the charm which she found in their conversation and companionship alleviated her troubles. These three hearts were soon moulded into one, filled by the same feelings and moved by the same inclinations. Elizabeth's new condition was perhaps too happy, and Our Lord did not fail to throw some drops of wormwood amongst the sweetness. Christopher Mora fell ill, and his father, Dr. Mora, a skilful physician, lavished upon him all the cares of his art. Seeing that his two daughters would not separate themselves from Elizabeth, and that Christopher's state required his constant assistance, he decided to unite the whole family in the same house. He hired a little apartment above that which he himself occupied, and ordered his son and daughter-in-law to establish themselves there. Elizabeth submitted to the authority of her father-in-law, left her splendid home in the Vespignani Palace, and installed herself in that which had been assigned to her. By this change she ceased to be mistress of her own house, and placed herself under the orders of her new parents. Her clear-sightedness made her foresee the many difficulties which would arise in such a delicate position, and in order to overcome them, she resolved to forget that she was a daughter-in-law, and to comport herself towards every one as if she were the youngest child of the family. Having once marked out for herself this line of conduct, she courageously embraced it, and never deviated from it. She was obedient and docile, and claimed for herself no authority over any one, not even over the servants. She was placed in the society of more than thirteen persons of different characters and modes of thought; she had to please all, to accommodate herself to all, to live in peace with one without giving offence to another; yet, by force of patience, humility, and meekness, Elizabeth succeeded in gaining the general esteem and love of the whole family.

She would certainly have been happy in this new position if the misconduct of her husband had not broken her heart. Instead of changing his conduct with the course of years, his evil passions only increased. His incomparable wife tried every means which the most sincere affection and the most ardent charity could invent to induce him to reform, but it was all in vain, and her efforts remained fruitless.

What conduced to render her cross intolerable was this—that Christopher's family ended by blaming her for all her husband's misconduct; reproaching her for living too retired a life, and for alienating his affection by the excessive austerity of her conduct. These reproaches were as unmerited as they were painful. Elizabeth studied all her husband's wishes and inclinations, and never refused him anything that could please or gratify him.

At a sign from him, she did not hesitate to accompany him to the theatre, which, in Rome, where the plays are proper and decent, is far from offering the same disadvantages as in other places. On these occasions, her pious sisters-in-law accompanied her, and there she could still enjoy their loving society. However, during all these troubles, she received a double consolation. The first was in the presence of one of her brothers, who came to reside in the house, in order to study medicine under Dr. Mora. The second was the liberty to live in solitude and increase her time of prayer. Being no longer mistress of the house, and having no household cares or domestic arrangements, she had many leisure hours. When Christopher Mora unreasonably tormented his virtuous wife, her brother defended her; and if sorrow overwhelmed her heart, she took refuge in God.

Elizabeth had brought three children into the world; the first and second had taken their flight to heaven very soon after their baptism; the third, a daughter named Mary Anne, still lived. She was with her mother in Dr. Mora's house. On the 5th July, 1801, another daughter was born, who was the youngest child of our Venerable Mother. The joy of the parents at the birth of this child was inexpressible. The baptism was celebrated with the greatest splendour possible, and the child received the name of Lucina, in honour of the Saint on whose feast she was born. A great happiness was always the signal of a new cross to Elizabeth. On the Feast of the Assumption she was attacked by a severe colic, which rapidly increased, notwithstanding all the care which Dr. Mora lavished upon her. To this dangerous illness another of a mortal nature was soon added. She was attacked by a malignant putrid fever—the *perniciosa* of Rome. All the aids of science were powerless, and our Venerable Mother was in danger of death when God Himself came to her assistance. He spread over her His merciful Hand, and when all human hope was over, rescued her from her extreme danger. The result of this frightful malady was to unite her more closely to Him, and to induce her to embrace the way of perfection with more courage and generosity. She herself related to her spiritual Father how Divine Grace then made itself felt. "This was," she said, "the last gift of Grace, which rescued me from the mortal lethargy in which my poor soul had been immersed. The thought of eternity, where I believed myself to be certainly passing, occupied all my thoughts. The grief which I experienced for my sins was excessive. All my hopes were in the merits of my crucified Jesus, whose image I held clasped in my hands. I consecrated myself anew to Him in life and in death. I sought only my Jesus; one only visit gave me pleasure, that of my Confessor. Given up by the physicians, I received the last Sacraments... Then, by the goodness of God, this illness began to leave me, and during the five months of my convalescence, my Confessor came frequently to see me. He led me to consider that the life which Our Lord had miraculously restored was no longer mine, but His. The words of His minister touched my heart. I offered myself entirely to Our Lord, and I began to go to Confession and Communion every week. At length, a desire to receive Holy Communion more frequently took possession of me; but, not daring to say so to my Confessor, I recommended myself to Our Lord and to the Blessed Virgin, so that they might inspire him. And, indeed, he one morning said to me: 'A particular inspiration obliges me to give you Holy Communion three times every week.'"

Elizabeth's Confessor, at this time, was the Rev. Father John James Pegna, an ancient Religious of the Society of Jesus, and Penitentiary of the Basilica of S. Peter, up to the time of the suppression of that Religious Order.

CHAPTER III

Elizabeth entirely changes her life and becomes quite docile to Divine Grace.—Her new style of Life brings about fresh persecution: Help accorded her by Our Lord and the Blessed Virgin.—Wonderful fruits which she draws from two Retreats.—Our Lord sends her a Director according to her own heart, the Rev. Father Ferdinand of S. Louis.

FROM this memorable period, Elizabeth showed herself entirely docile to Divine Grace; she renounced for ever all vanities and worldly pleasures. She threw aside the magnificent dresses with which she had loved to adorn herself, lived in the most profound solitude, and prolonged as much as she could her communications with Our Lord, the Blessed Virgin, and the Angels and Saints of heaven.

A change so remarkable in her manner of dress, and in her whole conduct, drew upon her a cruel persecution both from her friends and her whole family; her husband alone left her in peace, and allowed her to live according to her own tastes and inclinations. The sharp remarks which she heard, and the plausible reasons brought forward to induce her to return to her former style of living, made a profound impression upon her, and perhaps her constancy would have given way, if the Blessed Virgin had not come to her aid, and powerfully supported her in this violent conflict.

On the morning of the 7th September, 1803, whilst suffering from doubt and uncertainty regarding her new way of life, the Queen of Compassion appeared to her, holding in her hands and caressing in her bosom a dove, from which issued on all sides rays of light, and which bore under its wings marks of bleeding nails. One of these rays of fire struck the heart of Elizabeth, and made so severe a wound that she fainted away. When she recovered, she found herself completely changed; her heart was on fire, and in the excess of her transport she exclaimed: "At last, thou hast conquered, O holy love of my God!" The wound which she had just received in this vision of the heavenly Spouse had given her a violent palpitation. She feared lest any curious eye should penetrate the mystery of her illness, and begged of Our Lord the grace to keep His favours concealed from the eyes of men. Instantly the loving palpitation ceased, to return only at the time of prayer and Holy Communion.

The enemy of her soul, enraged at having sustained such a shameful defeat, subjected her to a more dangerous and perfidious assault. An ecclesiastic, whose dignity and character made him greatly respected, told her that she was mistaken, that she ought to leave to the inmates of the cloister such constant solitude and assiduity in prayer; that her duty was to please her husband, and give satisfaction to his family; and that in doing otherwise she made herself responsible for all the evil of his conduct.

This advice, emanating from so high a source, came upon Elizabeth like a thunderbolt. Almost beside herself, and not knowing which side to take, she hastened to throw herself at the feet of Our Lord, and implored Him to make known to her His Divine Will. Our Divine Saviour immediately appeared to her, and said: "My daughter, why do you grieve? Do you not remember that you are consecrated to Me?" Elizabeth was overjoyed at receiving at once so great a favour; but she felt that the words which she had heard concealed a mysterious meaning of which she had not the secret. Our Lord again said to her: "Remember that you are consecrated to Me." He repeated these words three times.

At the third repetition a ray of Divine Grace illuminated the mind of our Venerable Mother, and she recalled to mind the vow of perpetual virginity which she had made as a child in the Monastery of Cascia. At this remembrance she broke out into sobs, and going in all haste to seek her Confessor, she threw herself at his feet, overwhelmed by the weight of her infidelity. Her prudent Confessor consoled her by mild and charitable words. "My daughter," he said, "do not afflict yourself. You have not sinned in taking a mortal spouse, because you had forgotten your vow of virginity, and you have acted in all sincerity. You see that Our Lord Himself has had the goodness to excuse you, by assuring you that, notwithstanding your present condition, you are still consecrated to Him. For the rest, remain in peace, I will obtain a dispensation in your favour from the sacred Penitentiary."

This wise advice restored peace and serenity to the soul of Elizabeth; from that time she thought only of making more rapid progress in the ways of Christian perfection. It seemed to her that daily Communion would be necessary to surmount all the obstacles which opposed her heroic design. But in her humility she would never have dared to manifest such a desire to her spiritual Father; so that she again had recourse to the Blessed Virgin, and implored her to inspire her Confessor to grant her what she desired, if it were according to the Divine Will.

On the eve of the Immaculate Conception, Elizabeth was suddenly ravished in God, and in this state she saw defile before her a numerous and beautiful procession of Blessed Spirits. The Blessed Virgin closed the procession, carrying the Divine Infant in her arms, resting upon her bosom. On passing before Elizabeth she made a gracious sign, and gave her to understand that her prayer was heard. In fact, on Christmas Eve, her spiritual Father told her that an inspiration from God obliged him to admit her daily to Holy Communion. This was the first of an uninterrupted series of graces and favours of the highest order. Besides the miraculous Communions which she had the happiness to receive from the hands of the Prince of the Apostles, of the Angels, the Holy Eucharist became to her a centre and home of divine light. Our Lord one day taught her a method of living always in His presence, by adoring Him under the veil of the Holy Species in the Tabernacle. In order that she might put this in practice, He granted her three special graces, on condition that she should submit their use in obedience to her spiritual Father.

But nothing inflamed her with love for the August Sacrament so much as the following vision. Finding herself in adoration at the foot of the Holy Tabernacle, she was ravished in spirit, and saw her soul under the form of a temple, in which a majestic Altar was raised. S. Felix of Valois and S. John of Matha, appearing to her in the centre of this mysterious sanctuary, took with extreme reverence a Host from the Ciborium, and placed it on a paten of gold on the altar of her soul. At the same time, the Divine Host shot forth a luminous ray which went direct to her heart, and enkindled in it such ardent love, that she did not know how to bear it. S. Felix and S. John then united their spirit to hers, and offered it to the most Holy Trinity.

In consequence of this vision, Elizabeth conceived so great a devotion for the adorable Eucharist, that she concentrated there her most ardent affections; so that at the end of her life, when his Holiness Pius gave her permission to have Mass celebrated in her oratory, three times in each week, and there to communicate, the joy which she then experienced made her forget all her sufferings. She could not tear herself away, either by day or by night, from a place where Our Lord had so often appeared in a visible manner. We shall see, in the continuation of her life, that the greatest favours Elizabeth received were ordinarily granted her after Holy Communion. Our Lord frequently honoured her with His visits when she received the adorable Eucharist. Her Communions were so miraculous that the Venerable Mother herself knew not how to explain them. But our Divine Saviour cultivated in her especially the virtue of humility, the foundation of all other virtues, and the mystic salt which preserves all good works from corruption; so that she saw in herself nothing but defects.

One day Elizabeth saw furious devils under the form of giants rushing towards her, and trying to deprive her of life by piercing her throat.

On seeing this great danger, she cried out, and called Our Lord to her aid. At the same moment a ray of light, like lightning, flashed in the eyes of these hideous monsters, and immediately put them to flight. Elizabeth, being freed from these horrible phantoms, was pouring forth her thanks to God, when Our Lord appeared to her, and said: "You were already no more than a corpse without life, when I took compassion on you. If my mercy had not been so great to you, what would have become of you?"

Such words received from the adorable lips of our Divine Saviour enkindled in the heart of Elizabeth an extreme desire to labour more generously than ever in the work of her sanctification.

In order to second this impulse of grace she proposed to herself to make a few days' retreat in her own house. She succeeded in the execution of this pious intention in the course of the year 1804. She came out of it inflamed with love for God; and determined this time to show herself faithful to all her resolutions, she resolved to sign them with her own blood. But when she tried to draw blood for this purpose, she lost courage. At the sight of her own weakness, she prayed the Blessed Virgin to strengthen her. Then feeling her courage revived, she drew the blood, dipped her pen into it, and resolutely signed the formula of her new engagements. She then deposited it at the feet of the picture which, as we have related, had formerly preserved her from death. Her prudent Confessor, seeing such heroism, feared that his penitent would go to some pious excess if he left her to her own fervour, and resolved to subject her to a severe trial of obedience. He ordered her to burn before the same picture of the Crucifixion the paper which she had thus sealed with her blood. Elizabeth immediately obeyed, and to avoid all danger of illusion, she made a vow of obedience to her Confessor for a limited time.

Three years later, that is to say in 1807, she desired to make a second retreat. This time being at liberty, and mistress of her own time, she retired into the Monastery of the Infant Jesus, near Sta. Maria Maggiore, and there spent the nine days preceding the Feast of Pentecost. There she received graces of the highest order. Our Lord plainly revealed to her that He designed to make her a great Saint. He enriched her with the gift of extraordinary recollection, which enabled her to enjoy almost continually the sensible presence of her Saviour, and also that of the company of Blessed Spirits. These great graces enkindled in Elizabeth vivid flames of love. The transports which she experienced at length caused her strength to give way; and at the time of Holy Communion, she fainted away in public. On recovering, she made every effort to conceal the cause of her weakness; she even mildly complained to God that He had made her a spectacle before the eyes of every one.

At this time, another Father of the Society of Jesus, had replaced Father J. J. Pegna in the direction of this privileged soul. But her new Confessor, having become seriously ill, our Venerable Mother had sometimes occasion to speak to the Rev. Father Ferdinand of S. Louis, of the Order of the most Blessed Trinity; and profited by these opportunities to ask his advice regarding certain things which were passing in her soul. The words of this venerable Religious enlightened her mind, brought peace to her soul, and inflamed her love for God. Such marvellous effects led her to believe that Our Lord had probably chosen him to be the guide of her soul. She consulted her Confessor on this point; and his illness becoming more and more serious, he advised her to consult another Father of the Society, whom he mentioned, and to follow his decision. She obeyed, and this Father told her that her attraction proceeded from Divine Grace, and that she might follow it without fear. Elizabeth, no longer doubting the Will of God, went to throw herself at the feet of Father Ferdinand, and begged him to take charge of her soul, making a general Confession to him at the same time. This new director permitted her to renew every three months, for that space of time, her vows of chastity, poverty, and obedience. She was at liberty to bind herself by a vow of chastity, because her husband, continuing to lead a guilty life, had entirely deserted her. She also obtained a particular authority to apply herself to the practice of humility, so as to make more progress therein. Fortified with these permissions, which submitted all her actions to obedience, and thus doubled their merit, she made giant steps in the way of perfection.

Our Lord wished to show her how pleasing to Him were her docility, and the prudent directions of her spiritual Father. One day, whilst hearing the Mass of Father Ferdinand, she was ravished in ecstasy, and saw Our Lord take him and her and press both affectionately to His bosom; and after having fixed His eyes upon them both, He promised them salvation and eternal life.

CHAPTER IV

The Venerable Mother proposed as a model to Mothers.—She commences the education of her two Daughters from their earliest years.—She gives them a taste for reading holy books and teaches them to meditate on Eternal Truths.—She takes pains to form them to the virtue of patience under contradictions and sufferings.—Her eagerness in making them frequent the Sacraments early.—One of her Daughters decides on embracing a Religious Life, the other makes choice of the married state.

IT is now time to consider Elizabeth as a mother, applying herself to the duty of giving her children a pious education. The Christian mother, on reading the Life of a Saint who has carried away the palm of virtue in the career which she herself is following, desires to know how she has acquitted herself of the grave and painful duties which are attached to this beautiful title, the difficulties she has had to encounter, and the manner in which she has overcome them. On the other hand, those children who desire to advance in virtue, on reading these pages, will learn what they should be taught so as to avoid all snares, and how necessary docility is to defend them from the many dangers to which they are exposed by the inexperience of their age.

The serious illness of which we have spoken in a previous chapter prevented Elizabeth from nursing and bringing up her little baby, Mary Lucina. In order to give less trouble in the family, she requested her father-in-law to find a nurse for the child away from the house, as is frequently the custom in Italy.

On being restored to convalescence, the first use she made of her returning strength was to pay a visit to her infant, so that she might see for herself that proper care had been bestowed on it. What was her distress when she saw the carelessness, hardly to be credited, of the nurse! She found her child revoltingly dirty, and covered with vermin. Making an effort, she raised with the tips of her fingers the miserable couch which served for its bed, and was struck with horror at the sight. It was a mass of filth and impurity.

She took her little daughter away at once, and placed her with another nurse who had been highly recommended. Some time after she again went to see her, and her grief was this time not less bitter, for she found her child dying, as it were, of hunger, and so weak that she could no longer cry. This double experience took away from her any idea of trying another nurse. She brought her child home, and by means of the assiduous care which she lavished upon her, she rescued her, in the course of a few days, from the brink of the grave, and her health was soon restored. She also undertook the education of her eldest daughter, and associated the younger with her sister as much as possible.

Elizabeth, satisfied that she could not begin too early to inspire in her children a love of Our Lord, did her best to form the hearts of her two little daughters, and to train them in exercises of piety. From their most tender years, almost before they could speak, she gave them little lessons suited to their baby years. She had them constantly with her, and at favourable times read to them short stories drawn from the Holy Scriptures, or the Lives of the Saints. Her little girls listened to these pious recitals with marvellous attention, and never forgot her loving words and instructions.

An ardent desire to learn was developed in their young minds by these readings, and they were always asking questions of their mother. She took advantage of these occasions to teach them our August Mysteries, and all that our holy religion contains most adapted to touch their hearts. When they grew older, she read to them short meditations on the Four Last Things, and induced them to reflect, as it were, unknown to themselves, on these great truths.

Guided with so much wisdom, the two little girls were inflamed with the love of God, and often asked their mother how it was possible for them to please Him? She replied that this could be done especially by the practice of recollection and mortification. She taught them from that time to avoid boisterous amusements, and to impose upon themselves little acts of penance suitable to their age. She afterwards required from them an account of the manner in which they had performed their pious exercises, and the children, to satisfy their beloved mother, did all in such a manner as to give her great pleasure. On witnessing their touching fidelity Elizabeth could not contain her joy, and she assured them that their eagerness to do right was very pleasing to God.

No one knew better than Elizabeth how life is sown broadcast with trials, and how a soul needs generosity and patience in order to triumph over them. Her most constant care was to form this patience in the souls of the two little angels whose education Our Lord had confided to her. She had taught them so well to preserve silence, and never to show any resentment in the little trials which they met with, that at this early age they knew already how to bear the Cross with a submission and tranquillity astonishing even to those who have grown up under its shadow. At an early age Elizabeth presented her children to the Bishop, so that by the reception of the Sacrament of Confirmation they should be fortified by the Sacred Unction, and endowed with the gifts of the Holy Spirit. She did not wait till they were of a more advanced age to bring them to the Holy Table. When they had arrived at their ninth or tenth year she took them to the Monastery of the Infant Jesus, near Santa Maria Maggiore, and confided them to the zealous Religious of that house, to prepare them, by a holy Retreat, for their first Communion. Afterwards she took them herself, and had the joy of seeing them kneeling by her side at the Sacred Banquet.

When they had been once admitted to Holy Communion she made them regularly communicate every week. In order that such frequent Communion might not become wearisome to them or degenerate into custom, she allowed them to choose their own confessor, and taught them to use all the employments of the week either as a preparation for it or as an act of thanksgiving. The little girls were so well satisfied with the direction of the Rev. Father Ferdinand of S. Louis, the spiritual Father of their Venerable Mother, that they never wished to change. In the state of recollection in which they lived the Holy Communion had become the centre of their life, and the motive of their whole conduct. They received It with delight, and to have been kept away from It would have been a keen sorrow to them.

Our Lord blessed, in a visible manner, the course taken by Elizabeth with her daughters. Yet she still feared that she had not shown herself equal to the duties incumbent on every Christian mother. Her profound humility made her dread her own weakness, and she believed it to be her duty to procure another guide to supply her place. One day when she was in prayer before a picture of the Blessed Virgin, she suddenly fell into an extraordinary ecstasy. In the ardour which consumed her she called her two daughters; they immediately ran to her, and finding her with open arms, they threw themselves into them. Whilst she still held them affectionately pressed to her bosom, she fell upon her knees with them, and presenting them to the Mother of God, she said: "My Mother, I confide to you these two; I now renounce all claim as their mother; you will take them, and I shall be only their governess. I am incapable of being their guide, you will take my place. I am satisfied that in giving them to you, I leave them in good hands." Afterwards she often reminded her daughters that the Madonna was their true Mother, and that they ought never to lose sight of the solemn act by which they had been consecrated to her. This admirable mother took extreme care to guard these young hearts from all that might be likely to enfeeble the sentiment of Divine love. She never allowed any one to take them to the theatre or to any other worldly amusement. She had even the happiness to induce them never to take any part in the Carnival, which was in Rome, in old times, peculiar for the innocence and simplicity of its character. Dr. Mora's house was in the Corso, where the games take place; during the hours it lasted, Elizabeth would go out with her daughters and procure for them some amusement elsewhere. She also accustomed them, at these times when God is so much offended, to make more frequent visits to the Blessed Sacrament, and invited them to go oftener than usual to Holy Communion.

Dr. Mora had a large and splendid library. Elizabeth had taught her daughters that nothing is so dangerous as imprudent reading,

Chapter IV

and they were never allowed to take a book which they had not received from their mother's hands. She would also have wished to keep from their ears all frivolous conversations on the fashions, worldly news, gossip, and other follies; but this was impossible. She was deeply grieved because she was unable to find a remedy for an evil capable of paralysing the good of all her efforts.

There were many serious dissensions in the Mora family; the numerous persons who composed it did not agree among themselves; and moreover the husband of our Venerable Mother openly lived a scandalous life. Elizabeth knew how to take advantage of these scenes, which she could not conceal from the sight of her young daughters; and inspired by God, she was able even to draw precious advantages from these evils. She made her children understand that peace in families is the most valuable of all treasures; and induced them to use all their efforts to foster and maintain it in their own home.

She told them that to procure so great a benefit they must be gentle and forgiving themselves, never be angry with any one, never repeat ill-natured stories; but comply with the wishes of others, and give up their own wills. She taught them that imprudent reports are the greatest cause of discord among those who ought to be united and to love each other; and that it was therefore a most sacred duty to keep secret what they heard, and never to repeat anything which might possibly disturb or cause anger and heart-burnings. Faithful to this teaching, these two young girls were silent, and became as prudent in speaking as people who were far more experienced and advanced in age. It was still more difficult to stop their murmurs against their guilty father, who carried his passion and folly so far as to leave his family actually in want, in order to supply the extravagances of a person who covered him with ridicule and shame. Christopher Mora's conduct was inexcusable, so that his pious wife could not speak of it approvingly to her children. She had recourse to religious motives so as to ward off their resentment against their father.

She reminded them of the great commandment of Our Lord, which obliges us to honour our father and our mother, if we wish to have a part in eternal life. They were not allowed to lament over the privations which were often imposed upon them; she taught them on the contrary to accept them and adore the incomprehensible designs of Divine Providence, Who desired to try them and to make them imitate the patience which made great Saints. Jesus on the Cross eloquently told them that they must suffer if they wished to show themselves worthy of His love, and to console Him in His sorrows; He was their true Father, and He would never fail to assist them, if they suffered with patience and without offending Him.

These conversations often repeated, and which seemed to come from the mouth of an Angel as they listened to them, fell like a sweet balm on the hearts of these young children. They continued to love and to cherish their father as if he had fulfilled all his duties, and lavished upon him marks of the most sincere and tender affection.

Filled with admirable prudence, Elizabeth knew that to banish the *ennui* of young persons, it was necessary to keep them constantly employed, and to vary their occupations in such a manner that one should relieve the fatigue of the other. She had drawn up a small rule of life, in which every action of the day found its proper place without the one encroaching on the other. The hours of prayer were fixed; and those of innocent recreation and healthy play were not forgotten. In their leisure time, the children could, according to their inclinations, cultivate flowers, tame little birds, or animals, or enjoy any other innocent amusement to their heart's content. Their holy mother desired that their education should be complete, and that they should not be ignorant of anything which was proper for their position in life. She procured clever masters to supply what she could not teach them herself. They were likewise very well brought up as regards other kinds of a woman's education, their mother having engaged a pious and experienced mistress to perfect them in the art of embroidery and needlework. But nothing equalled her solicitude in keeping from them all dangerous acquaintances. She never left them alone in the house; but either took them with her to church, or chose those hours for going out when her governess could remain with them. It was necessary that one person should enjoy her entire confidence, who should be penetrated with the fear of God, so that she could confide them to her when all were obliged to go out at the same time. In the house she never lost sight of them. There wore some young medical students with Dr. Mora; Elizabeth regarded them as so many dangerous birds of prey to her tender doves. Extremely modest, she desired that her daughters should conceive a great love for this angelic virtue. They slept in the same room, but each had her own little bed. She herself occupied the next room to theirs; so that when they had gone to bed, the door was left open, and they were always under their mother's eye.

When they were grown up to a certain age, she informed them that it was her intention never to influence them in their choice of a state of life, and that they were free to embrace whatever course Our Lord inspired them with. The younger, Mary Lucina, said that she desired with all her heart to become a religious. Her mother was overjoyed, explained to her the grace which Our Lord had granted her, and urged her to return to Him a thousand acts of thanksgiving.

The eldest expressed a contrary opinion, and requested her holy mother to marry her without delay. Elizabeth replied that she was ready to second her desire, but that she must wait until a suitable person presented himself. Incredible as it seems, the child protested that she would be married immediately; and the ardour which she manifested to enter a state of which she knew nothing but the name, was such that she fell dangerously ill. The distressed mother urged her to address herself to God so as to obtain what she desired. She herself offered up fervent prayers for the same intention. One day, while she was pouring forth her heart to God in the Church of S. Charles, at the Four Fountains, her eyes rested upon a sepulchral stone, where she read the following inscription: "Here repose the ashes of Caroline Alvarez." At the same time she heard a voice, which said to her: "Pray for me to the Most High, so that I may soon enjoy His presence. If you obtain for me this grace, I promise you myself to procure for your daughter Anne the favour which you desire."

Elizabeth related to her Confessor what had passed, and asked him what she should do. The venerable Father told her to pray for the deliverance of this suffering soul. Elizabeth did not lose an instant; she passed almost the whole night in prayer, and the next day made a fervent Communion for her. At this moment the departed person appeared to her, resplendent with light, and took her flight to Heaven in her presence. She had not long to wait for the effect of the intercession of the newly blessed. To tranquillise the pious mother regarding her daughter's choice, Our Lord said to her: "It was My design that your daughter should marry. Fear nothing in this state, I will shield her with a bulwark which will preserve her from becoming the prey of the enemy." A few days later, a virtuous young man presented himself to ask for the hand of Signora Maria Anna Mora, and her parents joyfully accepted him. Our dear Mother had the consolation of knowing that her zeal in forming these young souls to virtue was pleasing to God. One day, whilst she was recommending to Him the salvation of these two dear souls, she exclaimed in the fervour of her prayer: "Oh! my Jesus, may they be wholly Yours!" Our Lord appeared to her and said: "These two souls are already Mine. They are so because you desire that they should be." She saw Him then take both and place them lovingly in His Heart. Happy mother, happy children! Another time, our Divine Saviour addressed to her these remarkable words: "One day your example will serve to confound many mothers who have not fulfilled their duties." There are mothers, even those who call themselves Christians, who are far from realising all the importance of the duties which are incumbent on them with regard to the children whom God has confided to their care.

Chapter IV

Perhaps the following anecdote may open the eyes of some: One Christmas night Elizabeth was meditating on the touching mystery of an Infant God being born in a stable, and laid upon the straw of a miserable crib. Her heart melted at the sight of so much poverty and suffering. Our Lord desired her to understand that the mystery of the Divine Birth contained many other sorrows which no one can understand. He appeared to her in the crib, with His tender body bruised, and all covered with blood. At this sight Elizabeth broke out into sobs, asking what had brought Him to this miserable state. An interior light shone into her soul, and made her understand that the fathers and mothers in this unhappy world, instead of forming their children to virtue, filled their hearts with vanity and the spirit of false maxims, thus persecuting through them Jesus in His cradle.

CHAPTER V

Elizabeth a model for unhappy wives.—Simultaneous deaths of her two sisters-in-law, with whom she had lived on the most affectionate terms.—She sells all that she is possessed of, to satisfy her husband's creditors.—Miraculous cure of her father-in-law.—Christopher Mora is confined in the Convent of SS. John and Paul.—He attempts the life of Elizabeth.—Cruel persecution of Elizabeth by her sisters-in-law in consequence of her husband's conduct.

THE Venerable Elizabeth Canori is the model of unhappy wives; and we must acknowledge that the number of those who resemble her is unfortunately only too great. When one sees a young bride on the day of her marriage, her face full of joy, a wreath of flowers upon her head, and adorned with ornaments of every kind, one is disposed to say that she is happy, and perhaps to think her portion on earth an enviable one; but if we were endowed with the spirit of prophecy, and if, looking into the future, we could see the misfortunes which often await her, we should be struck with horror, and shed tears of compassion for this victim adorned for the sacrifice.

Elizabeth was a striking example of these cruel and unforeseen deceptions. Being unable to bear the sight of the poverty and discord which reigned in her own family, she wished to marry, hoping that when once her own mistress she would be able to enjoy a little happiness. Heaven seemed to smile upon her wishes, and granted her a husband honourable and rich beyond anything she had dared to expect. Full of delight at this unlooked-for happiness she left her paternal home, and hastened to enjoy the substantial advantages which fortune gave her, and the pleasures belonging to a free and independent position.

But, alas! this happiness vanished almost immediately, and what followed became more and more distressing. Elizabeth's first unexpected trial was her husband's jealousy, which obliged her, during ten months, as we have said, to remain a prisoner in her own palace. A second grief which pierced her heart more cruelly was the infidelity of a husband whom she tenderly loved, and who after having loved her with a most restless jealousy ended by despising her and leaving her entirely deserted.

This illustrious martyr of conjugal fidelity having thus entered on the way of Calvary, we will follow her step by step to the consummation of her sacrifice, and admire the triumphs of her heroic patience.

When Our Lord chooses a victim to raise her to the dignity of His crucified spouse, He begins by placing her in a kind of isolation from all creatures, so as to deprive her as it were of all sources of terrestrial consolation. It was in this manner that He treated Elizabeth. Her two sisters-in-law, who had come to live with her, had been more to her than all others; they entered into her feelings, shared in her afflictions, and gave her the example of every virtue. What more could be required by a pious and devoted soul, who, after all, aspired only to eternal happiness? Yet God showed Himself jealous even of these human supports, and he called to Himself her two holy companions almost at the same time. The blow was cruel, but the results were most advantageous to her.

Our virtuous Mother was left alone and uncared-for, exactly at the time when she required the most powerful protection. Christopher Mora was drawn by the devil into an excess of passion so blind, that his conduct became almost incredible. In order to gratify the avarice of the object of his madness, he did not scruple to leave his wife and his two angelic children in utter misery. He became so extravagant, that his ruin was complete, and he was obliged to declare himself a bankrupt.

The Mora family, on such an occasion, ought, it would seem, to have surrounded their unfortunate daughter-in-law with kindness and affection; at least, they should have aided her in drinking this bitter chalice. They took an opposite course, and in the midst of her troubles they overwhelmed her with incessant and unjust reproaches. To listen to them, she alone was the cause of all these misfortunes; she alone had brought about the dishonour of their house! To these unmerited accusations Elizabeth heroically submitted, adored the incomprehensible designs of Our Lord, and studied how to repair the evils of which she was entirely innocent.

In order to calm the irritation of the family, she resolved to give up all that she had to meet her husband's debts. She generously sold all her jewels, and even the valuable furniture of her own rooms. She restricted her expenses, and courageously embraced poverty and all the privations which accompanied it. When she had collected together all that she could realise, she had scarcely enough to pay half of what was owing. In addition to the voluntary sacrifices which she had imposed upon herself, she had the humiliation of being obliged to go herself to the creditors and implore them to be contented with the little she had to give them. Before undertaking these painful visits she purchased a small crucifix to take with her wherever she might go. She afterwards acknowledged that if she had not furnished herself with this powerful aid, her courage would have failed, and she would not have been able to submit to such a long series of humiliations.

Fortified with the sacred sign of her Lord dead upon the Cross, she set out, uniting herself in spirit with Our Lord dragged before the various tribunals of Jerusalem. She called upon all the creditors, one after the other, and spoke to them with so much modesty and gentleness that they were deeply affected. At the sight of this young lady, who had given up all that she had of any value to save her husband's reputation, they were softened, and were eager to accede to her request. There was one of them who, transported with admiration, conceived for her a criminal passion, and offered her, if she would only consent to enter into his views, to cancel her debt and give her his whole fortune. At this proposal Elizabeth put on so grave and dignified a countenance, and replied with so much firmness, that the imprudent suitor was silenced, and became confused and ashamed of his behaviour.

Conduct so magnanimous on the part of his incomparable wife should have touched the heart of Christopher Mora and recalled him to the practice of his duties. However, it was not so. He plunged yet further into the depths of folly and extravagance. After ruining his home, robbing his pious wife, and reducing his two daughters to poverty, he determined to satisfy the avarice of the object of his passion by appropriating the property of his own father. One day he secretly robbed him of a considerable sum. When Dr. Mora discovered that all this money was gone, he fell down from an apoplectic stroke.

On hearing of this sad event, Elizabeth hastened to the feet of Our Lord, and begged him with so much fervour to restore the health of her father-in-law, that she was heard. The doctor was restored to life, and in the course of a few days, recovered his former vigour. However, the detestable crime of Christopher Mora had terrible consequences for Elizabeth. She had offered herself to God as a victim for her unfortunate husband; and it seemed that she was to bear the consequences of all his guilty acts. Christopher's sisters conceived the idea of having recourse to Ecclesiastical Authority, to oblige him to break off the connection which occasioned so many evils. They had the right to do this according to the Canonical laws of the Pontifical States. When any member of an honourable family dishonours it by the public scandal of his life, the others are allowed to have recourse to authority against him, which, in such a case as this, obliges the delinquent to be imprisoned for a longer or shorter time in a Religious House, so as to give himself up to reflection and prayer, and to find leisure to reconsider his conduct. Such a punishment can evidently only proceed from the paternal spirit of the religion which presides over the government of the common Father of the Faithful. But the Misses Mora at the same time conceived another project, scarcely imaginable; this was to imprison also the Venerable Mother; and they dared to choose as the place of her retreat, a House of refuge for women of abandoned life. This step would have for ever compromised Elizabeth's reputation, and exposed her as a guilty woman in the eyes of the public. She understood this perfectly, but satisfied to meet the ignominy, she replied to this proposal, when made to her: "I will go wherever Our Lord pleases." But God did not suffer her to submit to this infamy, and He disposed events in such a manner that this odious

Chapter V

design was not carried out. However, the application was made for her husband, and, by order of His Eminence the Cardinal Vicar, Christopher Mora received the order to go into the Convent of SS. John and Paul, on Monte Cœlio. Here he passed a certain time, but instead of profiting by his sojourn in this house, he was enraged beyond measure at the course taken against him. Signora Mora, his mother, not being able to believe in all the wickedness of her son, and hoping that he had come to a better mind, pleaded his cause with her husband, and obtained his recall to the paternal home.

Returned to his family, Christopher became a furious devil, and there was no ill-treatment to which he did not subject his virtuous wife. He went so far as to require her to give him permission in writing to continue his former course of life. Elizabeth replied, that such an act on her part would be a crime, and that she preferred death a thousand times to becoming guilty of it.

Finding it impossible to bring her over to his views, he changed his tactics; he told her that he did not wish for this writing to enable him to return to that woman, but to repair his compromised reputation. Elizabeth did not agree to this demand, any more than to the first. Her husband then signified to her that she must either give him the writing which he asked for, or prepare herself to die by his own hand. Such a threat in no way shook our heroine, Elizabeth. Christopher, furious at her invincible firmness, seized a dagger, and threw himself upon her to execute his threat.

In this extreme peril, she fell on her knees, recommended her soul to God, prayed for her murderer, and courageously waited for the blow to be struck. At this moment God came miraculously to her aid. Her husband suddenly found himself seized with terrible fear, and deprived of all his strength. Frightened at such a visible chastisement, he threw himself at the feet of his victim, and asked her pardon. This she granted at once, prayed for him, and his strength immediately returned. But this man had yielded only to terror, and his heart was unchanged. Scarcely had he seen himself delivered from danger, than he overwhelmed his worthy wife with insulting and outrageous words.

Under the influence of his diabolical passion, he devised another stratagem to arrive at his infamous purpose. He openly declared to his family, that since Elizabeth refused him this writing, he was determined to put an end to his life by suicide. This was a perfidious measure, and partly obtained its effect. The family were alarmed, and Signora Mora herself, forgetting at this moment her habitual ideas of virtue and piety, begged her daughter-in-law to accede to the desires of her husband, so as to avoid this horrible misfortune. Elizabeth was astonished to hear such language from the lips of her respected mother-in-law, but she remained unshaken. However, Heaven saw this battle betwixt virtue and the devil, and helped Elizabeth to gain a glorious victory. She has herself described the help which she received in this terrible struggle. Her words are worthy of remark, and prove once more how God assists those souls who have the generosity to give up everything for Him, even their lives.

"My heart," she said, "was incapable of fear. Being always absorbed in God, I enjoyed an ineffable union with Him. My husband might have torn me into a thousand pieces, I should not have felt it."

This conflict lasted for an entire month. The Rev. Father Ferdinand of St. Louis, her Confessor, finding that this state of things had become intolerable, advised her to ask for a legal separation. But, at the same time, knowing that the ways of God as regards His Saints are impenetrable, he ordered her to pray most fervently to know His adorable Will. Elizabeth, docile as a child to the orders of her spiritual Father, obeyed without delay. Our Lord thus replied to her: "I desire you not to abandon these three souls, those of your husband and your two children, because I wish them to be saved by your means."

She then wrote the following lines to her Confessor: "Lay aside all thoughts of separation. I prefer the salvation of these three souls to my spiritual comfort. It is more advantageous to the glory of God to co-operate in the salvation of these three souls; and this will place no obstacle in the way of my perfection."

Thus, then, our Venerable Mother resolved to remain upon the battle-field, and not to leave it except by a glorious victory. Her heroic courage at last procured for her this triumph; but she purchased it by three months of terrible and incessant struggles. The powerful arms which served her, after prayer and the practices of penance, were silence, humility, and unalterable patience.

The lives of the Saints upon earth are generally war without a truce; scarcely have they vanquished one enemy than another presents itself.

As soon as Elizabeth was at peace with her husband, her sisters-in-law began to attack her, and made her submit to a cruel persecution. They were so blinded by their anger as to accuse her of being the sole cause of her husband's misconduct; they treated her as a false devotee, and spared no means of annoying her. Dr. Mora, being unable to rely upon his son's honesty since he had committed the theft of which we have spoken, confided the management of his house to one of his daughters, whose character was hard and capricious. It is useless to relate all the humiliations to which she made our Venerable Mother submit. But what more cruelly grieved this tender mother was to see her innocent daughters also harshly used, and often, without reason, beaten and struck. To increase her misfortune, she had not even a single room to herself, or a solitary place where she could be at liberty to open her heart in prayer. She had asked for, and with great trouble obtained, the top of a staircase, where she could conceal herself when Our Lord ravished her in ecstasy, so as not to be exposed in this condition to the sight of the whole family. The apartment which served as her bedroom was a place of passage; she could not remain there during the times when she was overpowered by the favours of Heaven.

Hell envied her even this wretched corner where she could converse freely with her God. One of her aunts, perceiving that she rose early, had made this a subject of conversation. The family were even on the point of forbidding her taking from her sleep the time for prayer which she could not find during the day. She lovingly complained to Our Lord, Who consoled her, and said: "I have permitted them to give you this open room so as to exercise your patience, and enable you to give a good example to all in the house."

Elizabeth submitted to everything so as to pacify her sister-in-law. She even condescended to fulfil the most simple domestic offices in the household; but nothing could satisfy this prejudiced person, and our venerable Mother received only the most bitter reproaches in return for her devotion. This wicked woman carried her cruelty so far as to tell her that she would no longer provide for her expenses or those of her daughters, and that from that time she must herself procure the necessary means for her own support and theirs. Elizabeth submitted to this hard proposal, and considered how to find the means to comply with it. She saw no other way of doing this, but by undertaking some manual labour; she procured shirts to make for the warehouses, and her industry was such that she completed three or four every day. It might have been expected that this austere sister-in-law would have been touched at seeing her descend so meekly from the noble rank in which she was born to the condition of a simple seamstress. But it was not so, and she placed no bounds to her inhuman behaviour.

One day, in the year 1812, she ordered Elizabeth to seek another residence, saying that she would no longer let her remain in the paternal home. She gave as her reason that Christopher's creditors continued to come and annoy their father, and that, as they had contracted the debts, it was just that they should support the unpleasant consequences. All that she would grant her, in her father's name, was to come and dine everyday at the family table, leaving her to procure as she could, at her own charge, the other daily meals. Elizabeth accepted without a murmur, and submitted to these new orders. She came every day with her two children to dine at her father-in-law's table, and took away with her wine, bread, and what was necessary for supper. Her mother-in-law, who loved her exceedingly, did her this favour unknown to the doctor, who was opposed to it.

Thus our Venerable Mother, who had formerly lived in comfort and luxury, saw herself reduced to carry away secretly the most common necessaries of life; and yet considered herself happy, saying that these trials were useful to her, by giving her further opportunities of humiliation.

CHAPTER VI

Death of the father-in-law of our Venerable Mother.—Elizabeth is expelled from the house of the Moras.—She miraculously saves her husband's life.—Extreme affliction caused by her own daughters.—Our Lord assists her in her poverty.—Wonderful history of a picture of Jesus of Nazareth.

THE 25th of August, 1813, was a day of sorrowful memories for Elizabeth. Dr. Mora had passed to a better world, and left his virtuous daughter-in-law in a strange position. During the days of mourning the family thought only of their affliction, and the cruel loss which they had sustained; afterwards they began to examine their affairs, and to consider in what manner they should divide the inheritance of the departed. The Misses Mora consulted together, and agreed to separate themselves entirely from their brother, and cease to give him even the miserable dinner for which they made him pay by so many humiliations.

According to their custom, they did not speak to their brother, but announced their determination to Elizabeth. They communicated two things to her at the same time: first, that she should for the future regard herself as a stranger to them, and seek another home; secondly, that as her husband had wasted his inheritance he should not participate in the paternal property. They offered to return her the amount of her fortune, and told her that her husband should provide for his family by means of his profession as a barrister. Elizabeth listened quietly to all this, and meekly said: "Very well; I will endeavour to find a house with a small rent, and will arrange for myself as well as I can." Her sisters-in-law showed themselves insensible to these beautiful and touching words; but this was not the case with the worthy widow Signora Mora. She greatly blamed the conduct of her daughters, and protested that if she could have done so, she would have left them at once to go and live with her daughter-in-law.

Elizabeth took a house at a low rent, and arranged in it the little furniture she had with perfect order and good taste, drawing up for herself a rule of life which permitted her to give herself entirely to God. She would have ended by becoming happy in this solitude, if her unfortunate husband had not given her fresh trouble. This man, blinded by his passions, had at last ended by leaving his wife in peace; but far from changing his life or his conduct, he had only plunged himself deeper into the abyss. He surrounded himself with wicked men, who drew him into attending their infamous meetings. Elizabeth warned him of the dangers into which he was running, but Christopher never took any notice of her wise remonstrances. To all that she said he only replied: "As for you, your only pleasure is to be always in church; do you wish every one to do the same?" However, Our Lord one day said to her: "If your husband does not at once withdraw from these abominable societies where My Divine Majesty is daily outraged, I shall punish him with death." The Venerable Mother, frightened by this terrible threat, implored Christopher to separate himself quickly from these perverse companions, if he wished to save his life. But her persuasions had no effect. It was necessary that this man should see the danger with his own eyes before he would believe it.

One day Elizabeth was in prayer when Our Lord said to her: "Run in spirit to the aid of your husband, who is on the point of receiving a mortal wound." At that moment one of the members of the infamous secret society, which Christopher believed to be so innocent, was waiting in a lonely place to kill him as a traitor. This would have been the fate of the obstinate husband if, by a miraculous power, the Venerable Mother had not come to his assistance and arrested the arm of the assassin. Whilst yet in a state of partial ecstasy, Elizabeth called her children, and said to them in an agitated tone of voice: "Come, my daughters, and let us give thanks to God. Your father has been in danger of death, and the Divine Mercy has spared him."

A few moments later, Christopher, quite distracted, came into the house. The fright which he had experienced brought on a fever, and he became dangerously ill. Elizabeth lavished upon him every care and attention to relieve his sufferings; the most tenderly

Chapter VI

loved wife could not have shown more affection and devotion.

Christopher, believing himself to be on the point of leaving this world, and going to render to God an account of his guilty conduct, consented to make his confession and reconcile himself to God. His holy wife, rejoiced at seeing him return to his duties, asked for his recovery from God, and obtained it so soon, that every one regarded his cure as miraculous.

Scarcely had Christopher recovered his health, however, than he again forgot all his good resolutions, and returned with all his heart and soul to the creature who had ruined him. In vain did the Rev. Father Ferdinand of S. Louis unite his efforts to those of Elizabeth, exhorting him to abandon her who had been the cause of all his misfortunes; he would listen to nothing.

After all these afflictions, it would seem that there could be no new ones, and that the patient Elizabeth had exhausted the chalice of sorrows. But this was not the case.

We have seen that up to this time each member of the family had brought, in turn, some drop of gall to embitter poor Elizabeth's cup; her daughters alone had remained faithful, and had shown themselves angels of consolation to her. Elizabeth watched them grow up with delight, and when overwhelmed with sorrow, they were the sole consolation of a heart so cruelly tried. But now Our Lord seemed, as it were, jealous of this sweet support, and wished to convince her that every creature is weak, vain, and inconstant. The circumstances which are now to be related are instructive: they teach Christian mothers never to reckon entirely upon the virtue of their children, but to guard them unceasingly from the perils to which they are exposed by their inexperience of evil, and the laxity of the age.

In consequence of hearing their Venerable Mother so continually blamed by the family, the Misses Canori Mora at length partly lost the extraordinary esteem which they had had for her. Having come to a certain age, and their establishment in life having been delayed by family circumstances, they had adroitly procured the means to see a little of what passed in the world, and the kind of life led by other persons of their age and position. They began by considering the reserve which she had imposed upon them as exaggerated, and in order to diminish the weight of the light yoke she had laid upon them, they relaxed in their practices of piety, and soon those exercises which had been their delight, became irksome to them. Their imprudence went still further. Some officers had a lodging opposite their house, and these girls were not afraid to show themselves often at the window, and even to invite a correspondence. Their mother was too vigilant not to see the deplorable change which was taking place in her two children. Their preoccupied air, and their desire for amusement struck her; but she was far from suspecting all the danger of the plots which had been secretly laid for them. At last these imprudent children carried their folly so far as to agree with these men to leave their home on a certain day and contract with them clandestine marriages. The day and the hour were fixed, and during the night the elopement was to take place. But Our Lord had compassion on them, and deigned to come to their aid at the decisive moment. He designed to try their mother, but not to give her a mortal blow. He Himself revealed everything to Elizabeth, and at the moment when the villains believed they were about to carry off the two children (for they were nothing more) their mother presented herself. The girls, seeing their opportunity lost, remained in their room, and took care to seem to know nothing about it.

The next day, however, their sorrowful mother called them to her, and believed it her duty, by grave and gentle words, to make them understand how great was their fault, and the danger they had so nearly incurred. The girls were exceedingly confused when they saw that their secret was discovered; but something more was required to make them enter into themselves, and this Our Lord granted. In speaking to them, their tender mother could not conceal her grief, and at last, seeing them untouched by her words, she fell down in a fainting fit, which looked like death. At this sight the imprudent girls felt as if they would die themselves, and

Chapter VI

a heartrending scene took place. The mother revived, and the two children did not know how to do enough to console her and reconcile her to life. Elizabeth in her turn consoled them, took them to their Confessor, made them reconcile themselves to God, and all was forgotten. From this time the two girls returned to all their pious practices, renewed their former fervour, and showed themselves more exemplary than ever. Their fault was turned to their advantage by the generosity with which they repaired it. But the state of poverty to which they were reduced was insupportable to them, and they could not patiently submit to it. Their father, Christopher Mora, took all that he earned from his lucrative profession to the adulterous woman of whom we have all along spoken, and left his own family to pine in want and indigence. The two girls saw the consequences of his conduct, and it was difficult to stop their complaints.

Their virtuous mother mildly reproved them, and exhorted them to make their material privations turn to the profit of their souls. She recalled to their minds the poverty of the Holy Family, and tried to inspire them with courage by teaching them to unite their sufferings to those of Jesus, Mary, and Joseph.

Providence, however, did not desert this sorely tried family; and Elizabeth, who had placed all her confidence in God, often proved that she had not counted upon Him in vain. Although she had not spoken of her poverty to any one, many persons in succession came to her aid, who, influenced by a Divine inspiration, arrived at the opportune moment to bring her the necessary help. This consideration on the part of our Lord filled her with such sweet consolation, that she forgot her most cruel troubles. God, whom she served with so much generosity, wished to make her a return, and to provide for her with a bounty worthy of His munificence. He began by making her feel His presence interiorly, and by sustaining her hope whilst waiting until the hour of His liberality arrived. One day her daughters were working with her, and showed their sorrow and resentment for the distressing carelessness of their father. Suddenly Elizabeth, inspired by the Spirit of God, exclaimed, "O my daughters, if you show yourselves virtuous and faithful, you will see what Our Lord will provide for you! Within a year you will be happy. God Himself will be your Father."

Notwithstanding the confidence which they had in their mother, they dared not more than half rely upon this great promise. However, they did not then understand its meaning, though the events which followed dispelled their doubts.

On the 7th July, 1816, on a Sunday, Elizabeth went to Holy Communion, and being absorbed in acts of thanksgiving, she heard the voice of her Beloved saying to her: "I shall Myself, to-day, fulfil for you the office of Father and Master. From this time forward you will have not only what is necessary for yourself and your family, but also what is superfluous." Elizabeth joyfully returned home, and had scarcely entered her house, when a holy priest, named Andrew Felici, whom she had never known, arrived from Imola. This holy man said to her:

"Whilst I was praying in the Basilica of S. Peter, a very clear voice told me to come and offer you a miraculous picture of Jesus of Nazareth, which I bring with me."

At Rome and in Italy Jesus of Nazareth is the name given to the "*Ecce Homo.*" Many of these holy pictures are miraculous, and give signs of life in any important crisis. In 1863, we were ourselves contemplating a picture of this kind in the church of Montecelli at Rome, which opened its eyes and raised them to Heaven with a sad and suppliant air. This fact, moreover, has been published in several religious journals. The pious priest, Andrew Felici, related to Elizabeth the miraculous origin of the picture which he had brought as a present to her. He was the Director of a young man in whom he believed he had seen precious gifts of Divine Grace. In order to put this opinion to the test, and to assure himself by a sign of the truth of these favours, he ordered him to paint for him three miniatures: one of "Jesus of Nazareth," another of "Our Lady of the Seven Dolours," and the third, "the Blessed Virgin with the Divine Child in her arms." Although the young

Chapter VI

man was ignorant of the art of painting he set to work to execute the order of his Confessor, full of confidence in the virtue and power of holy obedience. God blessed his great and simple faith, and he carried to his Confessor three very well executed miniatures. The good Father then added: "I have offered the picture of 'Our Lady of the Seven Dolours' to His Holiness Pius VII. I ask you to accept the gift of 'Jesus of Nazareth,' since He has Himself chosen your house for His dwelling-place."

Elizabeth had never before been so happy; she understood that her God had come to establish Himself as Father and Master of her home by means of this miraculous picture. She had it placed in a frame, raised an altar for it, and from that time she and her daughters made their devotions before it every day of their lives.

CHAPTER VII

Our Lord cures a sick person by the mediation of the Venerable Mother.—John Sala provides for the wants of the house, and is regarded as the father of the family.—Miraculous cure of Mary Anne Mora.—Elizabeth receives the gift of miracles.—History of several striking miracles.—Extract from the proceedings concerning the cure of Pius IX.

OUR adorable Saviour was yet to accomplish the second part of His promise; and to display his power in the house of His faithful servant Elizabeth. He did not delay long in showing that His grace had accompanied the miraculous picture. Two days had scarcely elapsed, when a dying person was recommended to Elizabeth's prayers. Full of faith, she replied: "Let us recite three *Credos* before this holy picture." All knelt down and recited the appointed prayers. The Venerable Mother then presented some pastry to Jesus of Nazareth, and prayed Him to bless it. She gave it to the person who had come to ask the aid of her prayers, and said to her: "Be assured that as soon as the sick person has eaten some of this pastry he will be cured;" and all happened as she had foretold, to the amazement of the physicians who surrounded the dying man.

On seeing this miracle, Elizabeth's two daughters began to hope that Our Lord would take pity on them, and rescue them from their poverty, as their venerated mother had predicted. This confidence was not in vain. One day, a wealthy man, named John Sala, called upon Elizabeth, and said that he wished to consult her upon the state of his soul. The Venerable Mother cordially consented. The conversation being ended, the gentleman said, "Madam, allow me to see your daughters." Elizabeth immediately called them. Signor Sala said to them: "Our Lord has made known to me that I must take the place of a father to you. Therefore, I shall pay you, beginning from today, a monthly pension. And further, you will have the goodness to address yourselves freely to me in all your wants, absolutely as you would to your own father."

So great was the astonishment of the two girls, that they scarcely dared believe in such good fortune. Recovered from their agreeable surprise they did not know how to express their gratitude. Their joy was so much the greater, because their mother's prophecy was accomplished; they could now better understand the favour which Heaven had granted them in giving them a mother so filled with the Spirit of God and His precious gifts. Signor Sala, having looked at the picture of Jesus of Nazareth, said that the poor Altar on which it was placed was not worthy of so holy an object, and that he would procure another more suitable. Soon after he ordered a very handsome frame of silver gilt, which may still be seen with Mother Mary Josephine Mora, Superior of the Oblates of S. Philip Neri, in the Square Dei Monti.

In the following year, 1817, another miracle was accomplished by the holy picture of Jesus of Nazareth, in Elizabeth's own house.

Mary Anne Mora, the eldest daughter of the Venerable Mother, had become consumptive. Her disease had already made great progress when her prudent mother judged it necessary to separate her from her sister, and place her in a separate room. Signor John Sala charitably and generously took as much care of Mary Anne as if she had been his own daughter. To procure for her some amusement, and cheer her gloomy thoughts, so as to prevent her dwelling too much upon her condition, he proposed to her to have the room which she occupied furnished according to her own taste. Mary Anne, very much pleased, fancied a very curious style of decoration. She ordered the upholsterer to adorn her room with columns and pillars in such a manner that when the work was completed the room should resemble a church rather than a chamber. In the meantime the pious mother gently exhorted her daughter to patience, teaching her the value of suffering, and how sweet it is in sorrow to leave one's self entirely in the hands of Divine Providence. For her own part, she incessantly recommended this child to God, and begged of Him the restoration of her health.

When the upholsterer began the work, the sick girl was in the last stage of exhaustion; but as the work progressed, her condition improved, and when all was completed, she had entirely recovered.

Chapter VII

She was able to get up some days before the end of the week, and when the last touches had been put to the work, she found herself quite cured. Nothing could express the happiness of this young girl, and the excess of her gratitude to Jesus of Nazareth. Her intense thankfulness inspired her with a thought worthy of her piety. She called her mother, and said to her: "Mamma, this room is not made for me; it might serve as a chapel for Jesus of Nazareth; I will gladly give it up to Him; it is just that I should do so, since He has cured me without remedies." Elizabeth could not hear these words without being deeply moved. She united her thanksgivings to those of her daughter, and joyfully entered into her pious designs. In this room, thus converted into a chapel, she had a beautiful Altar placed, upon which the Holy Sacrifice of the Mass was afterwards celebrated. From this time, the picture of the adorable Redeemer was placed there, and He made it a throne of goodness and mercy. One day, whilst the Venerable Mother was humbling herself in the presence of her Saviour for so many favours received, Our Lord said to her: "My daughter, all the favours which I have granted you up to this time do not suffice to express my love for you. I desire to grant you the gift also of miracles." At these words, the humility of Elizabeth was alarmed; she replied: "You know, O my God, that my desire is to live unknown in the world. Deign to grant these gifts to other souls who are more faithful to You."

Our Lord replied to her: "No, my daughter, I will enable you to work these miracles with the aid of My picture, and I will teach you how to do it. You may remain in peace; your love for a hidden life shall in no way suffer."

The number of miracles wrought by Elizabeth with the aid of this holy picture was incalculable. Rome, Albano, and Marino were literally filled. In Albano alone, where Elizabeth, during the last six years of her life went, on account of her infirmities, to pass the summer months, there were more than sixty sick, who were instantly cured, and were able on the same day to return to their usual duties.

Lands, up to this time barren and unfruitful, became fertile; and, what was yet more precious, the most obstinate sinners suddenly found themselves touched, and exhibited all the signs of sincere conversion.

The Venerable Mother took care to have always a vase full of water before the miraculous picture, so that Our Lord should bless it, and communicate to it His Divine virtue. She afterwards sent it to persons who asked for her assistance, and she accomplished these miracles in such a manner as to seem to take no part in them, and more than once without even being known.

We will mention some examples of these miraculous graces. The Venerable Mother often came to the aid of those who were dying in child-birth. The deposition of Anne Almini, an inhabitant of the town of Marino, is as follows: "At the end of the month of May, 1824," she said, "I was seized with the pains of child-birth at sunrise. I was not delivered at five o'clock in the evening. My sister Frances then gave me a cord with two knots, and the picture of Jesus of Nazareth, saying to me: 'The Saint who is in the house of Armati sends you this cord so that you may tie it round your loins, and she recommends you to have faith in Jesus of Nazareth, who will help you in your labour.' I bound this cord round me and kissed the picture which the Venerable Mother had sent me, and in a short time I was safely delivered."

Signora Mary Anne Vitali, of the same town of Marino, experienced symptoms of a dangerous pregnancy. In her distress she went to see the Venerable Mother, and recommended herself earnestly to her prayers. Elizabeth said to her: "You have reason to be anxious; the child which you bear is in a dangerous position. But take courage, you will escape without danger." Some time after she rose during the night, and called her daughter, and also Clementina Ercoli, and said to them: "Rise up, and go and pray for Signora Vitali, who is on the point of bringing her child into the world." They remained in prayer for a long time, then suddenly Elizabeth arose and said: "That is enough; Signora Anne Vitali is safely delivered." All these facts were afterwards proved to be true.

Chapter VII

Elizabeth also procured the grace of Holy Baptism for a child who, without her aid, would have been deprived of it. She often saw a woman named Mary Trentanni, and every time she saw her she said to her: "Recommend yourself to Jesus of Nazareth, because you have to pass through a critical time." Two years later this woman was unable to bring forth her child, and the grief of this Christian mother was intense at the thought that her child would be deprived of Holy Baptism. The Venerable Mother informed her that, if she would consent to undergo the Caesarian operation, the child would be found alive, and might be baptised. This courageous woman had strength of mind to request this operation to be performed as a real favour; her prayers were heard, the child was living, and before its death received the Sacrament which opened for it the gates of heaven.

The most serious maladies soon gave way before Elizabeth's heroic faith. Signora Anna Maria Desantis had the sorrow to see her husband attacked by a terribly malignant fever, which brought him to the verge of the grave. The skill of the physicians was powerless against the malady. The inconsolable wife wrote to the Venerable Mother to ask the aid of her prayers. Elizabeth sent her a picture of Our Lady of Good Counsel, a piece of the scapular of Jesus of Nazareth, with a prayer of S. Ignatius, and wrote to request her to place all these pious objects under her husband's head. Signora Desantis carefully did all she was ordered, and the sick man recovered his health so rapidly that the physicians could scarcely believe their own eyes. In another case where the sick person was in his agony Elizabeth recalled him to life with the same facility. The mother of Isabella Silvestri was reduced so low that the priest could not leave her, and was recommending her soul to God, whilst waiting for her last sigh. She hastened off to seek Elizabeth, and asked for some holy water from Jesus of Nazareth and the aid of her prayers. Before leaving, she said: "Do you believe that Jesus will grant us the life of my mother?" Elizabeth replied:

"I assure you that Jesus of Nazareth will cure her out of regard for her poor children." Isabella flew home to her dying mother, made her swallow a few drops of the miraculous water, and from that moment she gradually recovered. This person thus rescued from the gates of death survived several years.

She also cured a dropsical woman in a manner no less marvellous. The mother of Angela Ferroni had grown so enormous that it was painful to her to put one foot before the other. Notwithstanding the difficulty she experienced in walking, she dragged herself as well as she could to Elizabeth, the refuge of all who had the happiness of knowing her. The Venerable Mother blessed her with the picture of Jesus of Nazareth, and after having made her drink of the miraculous water, said to her: "Take courage, you will infallibly be cured; moreover, Our Lord will grant you also the cure of your suffering daughter. But, I warn you, that this malady will return later, and that you will then die of it." From the evening of the same day the swelling diminished, and three days later this woman was so far recovered that she returned to her domestic occupations. Nine years afterwards the dropsy returned, and she then fell a victim to it.

Again, with the aid of Jesus of Nazareth, she delivered Vincent Martucci from frightful convulsions. From his youth, this man experienced convulsive attacks, which caused him to fall suddenly to the ground, deprived of sense, and frothing at the mouth. He was taken to the Venerable Mother, who placed upon his neck a scapular of Jesus of Nazareth, and made him drink of the water of the holy picture. From that very day Vincent Martucci had no more convulsions; he is still living, and enjoys perfect health.

The grace of bringing about reconciliations is a miracle more astonishing than the healing of the body, because it is a grace which must act upon the will and change it. Some one informed the Venerable Mother that in the house of Rose Terribile dissensions were frequent between the husband and wife. They were filled with such fury against each other that there was every moment great danger of fatal consequences.

Elizabeth took the picture of Jesus of Nazareth and went

herself to bless this house where the demon of hatred reigned supreme. It is worthy of record that from that time the husband and wife ceased their scandalous quarrels, and lived peaceably with each other. But the Venerable Mother accomplished another miracle which restored to health the immortal Pius IX., to whom the Church owes so many spiritual blessings. His Holiness, who was then only young Canon Mastai, was subject to epileptic fits. When they came on, he fell down as one dead, and gave signs of intense suffering. Elizabeth Canori Mora was the glorious instrument chosen by Our Lord to cure the future Vicar of Jesus Christ on earth. This event brought so much honour to our Venerable Mother, that we will give word for word the text of the miracle as it is recorded in the Judicial Process in Rome.

The witness on his oath deposed as follows: "Augustine Bartolesi, one of the principal employés of the Cameral Printing Office, led a holy life, and observed celibacy. When he had finished his daily occupations, he went in the evening to the establishment called Tata-Giovanni, and applied himself to works of charity among the young pupils who are there maintained free of cost. There he remained during the night, and I believe that he fulfilled the office of Prefect, doing all out of pure charity, and in order to procure a diminution of the expenses of this pious house.

"Young Canon Mastai was then Vice-Rector of the establishment. Seeing the sufferings which he endured, Augustine Bartolesi requested one of his sisters to entreat Elizabeth, whom she was in the habit of visiting, to pray for the Vice-Rector. 'It is very distressing,' he added, 'to see this worthy young Priest subject to these painful fits.' The sister of Augustine Bartolesi faithfully fulfilled the commission. Elizabeth replied to her: 'Let us go and pray to Jesus.' She afterwards brought her a small vial of water blessed by the holy picture, and said to her: 'Give this to Augustine, and tell him to put a little in the water or in the wine of the sick person, or even in his soup, and he may be certain that he will obtain the grace which he desires.'

"I believe that the Holy Father, who was then Vice-Rector, did not know anything about it. The result was favourable; after having tried the water, Canon Mastai only once again experienced these convulsions, and then they were very slight and scarcely felt. The gratitude of Augustine Bartolesi was inexpressible. He went himself to thank Jesus of Nazareth, and, being a charitable man, with a generous heart, he felt more happiness from this cure than if it had occurred to himself. Every one knew of the recovery of the young Canon; but, as they did not know how it had been effected, it was attributed to the blessing of Pius VII."

The witness whose words we quote is Mother Mary Josephine Mora, the daughter of the Venerable Mother. She has deposed as to what she had seen with her own eyes and heard with her own ears. And His Holiness Pius IX. frequently alluded to it.

CHAPTER VIII

The Venerable Mother is chosen to atone for the sins committed in her time, and to appease the anger of Heaven by her sufferings.—The devil is now permitted to make martyrs, and to take the place of tyrants and executioners.—Our Lord, in His goodness, forewarns His servants before they are given up to the temptations of Satan.—The Venerable Mother is prepared by symbolical visions for the battle against Hell.

ALL the afflictions which, up to this time, befell the Venerable Mother, have not passed out of the common and ordinary course. Many mothers might say, on reading this narrative, "I suffer as much as this Saint; it remains for me only to imitate her patience and heroic meekness." But Elizabeth was to fulfil a sublime mission, which, to satisfy the Divine Justice, required from her a martyrdom exceptionally severe.

In all times of universal perversion and sin, God is pleased to make choice of certain victims of predilection to discharge upon them the terrible effects of His anger, so as to be able to diffuse over the Faithful the sweet effusions of His love and mercy.

But, in order that a soul may be thus a reparatrix, and contribute to the general salvation, she must become as another Saviour upon Calvary and consent to bear the sufferings due to her guilty brethren. Formerly tyrants and executioners took upon themselves to cause these mysterious immolations, and, without knowing it, converted the world, by shedding the precious blood which appeased the Divine Justice. In these days, tyrants no longer having that power, Our Lord has appointed Satan to take their part, and fulfil their office. The Saints also, who have the mission of atoning for the sins of the world, and of opposing themselves to those who are inspired by the spirit of evil, fall, for a time, under the power of the devil, and are subjected to unheard-of cruelties. The "Annales de la Sainteté" of the nineteenth century will contain a great number of examples of this kind; and the story of Elizabeth Canori alone suffices to manifest this great truth.

But the Justice of God is never poured out upon a soul in all its rigour; mercy always precedes and accompanies it: if it were not so, who could support its terrible chastisements? So that one of the laws which Our Lord in His goodness seems to impose upon Himself, is to forewarn a generous soul of the trials to which she is to be subjected, so that she may strengthen herself by prayer, and prepare herself to sustain the severe combat which awaits her.

The life of the Venerable Mother is one of those in which this law of the supernatural and divine order is manifested. About two years after Elizabeth had given herself unreservedly to God, she was ravished in ecstasy and favoured with the following vision: She saw a very narrow and extremely steep road; and on the left, an abyss of horrible depth. She was ordered to go along this path on the slippery edge of the precipice. She hesitated, not understanding that this could be done without falling into the terrible abyss. Our Lord then appeared to her, and told her not to fear, that He was there to sustain her and direct her steps. He added, however, that He should withdraw His sensible presence at times, so as to see how she would behave in darkness and isolation.

This vision at first inspired Elizabeth with extraordinary confidence; but, afterwards, it gave rise to doubts, and she feared that she had been the sport of some diabolical illusion. Our Lord again appeared to her, and said: "My daughter, do you then know Me no longer? I am Jesus of Nazareth." At the same time He showed her the sacred wounds of His Passion. He also taught her, that to vanquish her enemies she had only to invoke His adorable Name. He then disappeared, and the Venerable Mother remained filled with happiness, and freed from her doubts.

A little later, Our Lord wished to make her understand what would be the nature of the enemies against whom she would have to fight. He again appeared to her, and caused an affecting scene to pass before her eyes. She suddenly saw an immense sea of great depth, and in the midst of its waves a small and frail boat. Our Divine Saviour ordered her to go on board this boat. She instantly

Chapter VIII

obeyed. He then gave the oars into her hands, and told her to cross this sea courageously, and try to gain the other side. He warned her that her enemies would come and pursue her, but that she should not be afraid, because with the aid of His grace she would triumph over them.

With a courageous heart and great confidence in God, Elizabeth boldly began to row and urge her boat towards the opposite shore. Scarcely did she find herself in the open sea, than she perceived a vessel full of men and devils who pursued her with great fury. But the sight of her numerous enemies did not alarm her. She invoked the Holy Name of Jesus, and as often as she repeated this Name, so terrible to Hell, the vessel was tossed about, and in the end it sank and disappeared in the abyss. She then intoned a canticle of thanksgiving in honour of her Beloved, and this vision rendered her more courageous than ever. Another time, she saw herself under the form of a gentle lamb in the midst of a sombre forest. This frightful place was filled with ferocious beasts, who regarded her as a certain prey. But she remembered that God was her strength, and called Him to her aid with reiterated cries. Our Lord hastened to her, and pointed out to her a retreat where these cruel animals did not dare to follow her. The Venerable Mother thus teaches us that the Refuge where the devil cannot enter is the adorable Heart of Jesus. According to the progress which she made in virtue, Our Lord prepared for her greater trials, which required more courage to overcome. But before exposing her to these dangers, He warned her of the coming trial by some new symbol.

One day she had a vision of a second road, more steep and rough than the first. In following it, she arrived at the borders of a lake filled with filthy water, and peopled by terrible animals, of which the sight alone was horrible. But she triumphed over all these monsters with the aid of confidence in God.

At one period of her life she experienced one of the most painful temptations which can assail a soul burning with love; she had to support an interior revolt against the Faith. These diabolical attacks were so violent, that she was afraid that she might fall into heresy, and so incur the hatred of God. Under this painful impression, Elizabeth seemed to have lost every feeling of happiness. She did not cease to weep for her sins and the sins of the whole world; and her eyes became the sources of inexhaustible tears.

This state of inexpressible torture arrived at such a pitch, that Our Lord took compassion on her, and came to console her. He appeared to her in the midst of her sorrow, and throwing at her a fiery dart, said to her: "My daughter, receive the impression of My love. This is not done by the ministry of an Angel, but it is I who desire to wound you with My own Hand. May the favour which I have shown you be a special proof of the love which I bear you." Fortified by this increase of love, the Venerable Mother entered a path yet more painful than that which she had hitherto traversed. The road which she followed was filled with thorns so thick and high, that she could not see either heaven or earth. Moreover, this place was infested by devils, who were laying deadly snares for her in the darkness.

She had recourse to Him Who is the strength of those who invoke His aid. Our Lord placed in her hands a mysterious staff, to enable her to find a path and victoriously fight the demons who came to assail her. Armed with this celestial staff, she set out on her road. It is impossible to describe the fatigue which she experienced during this journey, and the vexations to which she had to submit from evil spirits. But the danger did not end there; at a turn of the road she saw the passage intercepted by an impetuous torrent. How should she cross, without a bridge, such a violent current? She invoked Our Lord, and, touching a certain place with the end of the staff in her hand, she saw a miraculous plank fitted for a raft, on which she embarked, and full of confidence in Divine Providence, crossed safely to the other side.

Chapter VIII

Here she awaited the Will of God; she had overcome all obstacles and accomplished all that He had decreed for her; and the victory was complete.

Such solemn warnings repeated in so many ways foretold terrible struggles. The time has now come to describe some of them, and to show the truth of the words of the Apostle: "Those who desire to live godly in Jesus Christ shall suffer persecution."

CHAPTER IX

Elizabeth is given up to the vexations and cruelties of Satan, to appease the Divine Justice ready to chastise the world.—Unheard-of martyrdom which she endures during nine days and nine nights from the demons.—His Holiness Pius VII. delivers her.—She miraculously recovers her sight and her health.—The Blessed Virgin places the Infant Jesus in her arms.

S. TERESA said, that "the devil had received from God a power over her as he had in former times over the holy man Job." This was also the case with the incomparable woman whose life we are writing. There was no kind of torment to which Satan did not make her submit. If she desired to apply herself to prayer the tempting spirit came to trouble her, telling her that he would give her so many distractions that he would oblige her to give up the exercise. The Venerable Mother then had recourse to God, Who in a vision made her understand that He would never abandon her.

Our Lord appeared to her under the form of a young and beautiful Shepherd. She saw herself at his feet, as a faithful and obedient sheep. The adorable Saviour placed upon her forehead a sacred and victorious sign, in virtue of which it was impossible for the infernal enemy to triumph over her.

She sometimes experienced fits of strong inclination to anger and fury; but, notwithstanding the violence of the temptation, she remained mild and tranquil as if nothing had irritated her. Satan, furious at seeing that he could not alter her angelic character, appeared to her under horrible forms, and vomited over her such a volume of flame that she saw herself in the midst of an immense fire. But she remained at peace, and left Satan to act as he would.

More than once during prayer the devil enveloped her in a cloud of smoke so thick that it almost suffocated her. Once, on a fast-day, he gave her a factitious hunger so violent, that she felt that she could devour stone or iron. He made her examens of conscience so subtle and so extravagant, that she could see nothing but sin in all her actions, which threw her into an excessive fear of offending God. But again in this extremity she invoked God, Who dispelled her doubts, and, by a ray of light, confounded the spirit of illusion and falsehood.

Her Confessor, wishing to put an end to this continued war, ordered his penitent to command the devil, in the Name of Jesus, to leave her in peace. Elizabeth obeyed; and Satan seeing himself repulsed by the virtue of this adorable Name, withdrew, pouring forth a torrent of insults against the author of this salutary counsel.

Skirmishes of this kind were continual; but there were, besides, long and bloody battles. The horrors which we shall relate of one struggle may give us an idea of the fearful scenes which take place in Hell. It will show us to what a degree of heroism a soul may be raised when she is sustained by the Almighty power of Divine Grace.

In the beginning of January, 1819, Elizabeth took aside her youngest daughter, and spoke to her with great confidence. After dwelling on the favour Our Lord had bestowed upon her by calling her to a religious life, and the dangers from which He had preserved her, she informed her that if she were not yet allowed to enter her Convent it was on her account, so that she might assist her in her cruel infirmities. This daughter had already, according to an order from God, constituted herself her mother's secretary, and she took part in all the favours which were granted her.

She said to her: "You know, my daughter, that I must sustain a rude struggle against the infernal powers, and that the world will treat me as a fool. This struggle will show itself later under the appearance of an extraordinary malady. I inform you of it beforehand, so that you may know what you ought to do."

She afterwards related to her, that in the night of the last Christmas Festival the Blessed Virgin had appeared to her with the Divine Infant and S. Joseph. The Infant God cast upon her looks full of tenderness and love; but she wept bitterly, penetrated with the thought of her sins. In the transports of her love she offered herself to Him, and expressed to Him an ardent desire to suffer in

Chapter IX

order to please Him. The adorable Child then showed her the horrible chastisement with which He was preparing to strike the guilty world.

At this sight she offered herself as a victim of reconciliation in union with Our Saviour Himself. Our Lord consented to this, and informed her that she must prepare herself to sustain a terrible struggle against her enemies, but that she had nothing to fear, because He would Himself remain near her. She then adored the inscrutable decrees of the Most High, and united her will to the adorable Will of God. But afterwards, feeling herself frightened at the sight of the fearful sufferings which awaited her, she cried out to Jesus, Who again appeared to her, penetrated her with a ray of Divine light, and filled her with an invincible courage. After these words, she explained to her daughter the course she would have to take with the physicians and the members of the family. She also foretold to her that after this illness she would have two others, of which the latter, though apparently slight, would carry her to the grave. She told her how it would be necessary to treat her in all these various circumstances.

Two or three days later she called her two daughters begged them to assist her themselves, in the cruel trial to which she had to submit. She said, "Do not allow any other person to touch me. I shall be as docile as an infant in your hands. Our Lord will give you strength to support the fatigue night and day." The two young girls received this order from their Venerable Mother by shedding a torrent of tears; they threw themselves upon her neck, and promised her with all their hearts to do all that she had told them.

On the twenty-fourth day of the month of January, an interior light gave her to understand that the hour was come in which she must endure great torments for the Church, the Sovereign Pontiff, and all sinners in the universe. Our Lord appeared to her, and again assured her of His aid; He strengthened her by the assistance of a sweet odour which issued from His adorable wounds and inundated her heart with a celestial joy. When He had thus prepared her, He said to her, whilst showing her His wounds:

"Look, my daughter, at the great offences which are committed against My Majesty. If you love Me, offer yourself to My Divine Justice to repair them. Snatch from My all-powerful Hand the scourge with which I am ready to strike this ungrateful world, which provokes My vengeance and My fury. My daughter, I will be Myself your recompense."

At these words the Venerable Mother found herself transformed into another person. "Once fortified by Divine Grace," she said, "from being weak as a baby, I became terrible as a lion and full of courage. I went into the battle in the Name of the Lord."

The signal for the combat was not long delayed: God gave it from on High on the 25th day of January, dedicated by the Church to the miraculous conversion of S. Paul. The Venerable Mother was at that moment in prayer; she was surprised by a fainting-fit so serious that she seemed to have died. Her daughters found her extended on the earth, cold and motionless. They raised her, took her in their arms, and carried her to her bed. She remained in this condition for about twelve hours. Those who saw her thus believed her to be insensible; but the tortures to which she was subjected made her hair stand on end.

Several devils presented themselves to her, each carrying an instrument of torture, and threatening to torment her one after the other if she did not renounce her faith in Jesus Christ, and consent to all which they required from her. The holy woman renewed her confidence in Him Who giveth the victory in battle, and boldly said to them: "Torment me as much as you wish. I hope in Jesus Christ; in Him I am assured of victory."

At these words her enemies threw themselves upon her, and tormented her in all ways, saying to her: "We promise to leave you in peace, and make you happy on earth, if you will only deny the faith."

The intrepid martyr exclaimed: "I will confess the faith of Jesus Christ with my last sigh."

These diabolical monsters, animated by fresh rage at this heroic profession of faith, began to tear the whole inside of her mouth with very sharp iron points. Others violently opened her eyes, and poured into them boiling pitch. At each torture the invincible Christian renewed her act of faith. Ashamed to see themselves vanquished, these satellites of Satan began to apply a fire so violent and active to her whole body that the Venerable Mother believed that at each moment she must die of pain. The only relief which she experienced was in exclaiming: "I am a Christian; I adore Jesus Christ." These powerful words inspired her with marvellous strength, and placed her above all her torments.

At last these tortures were suspended; the Venerable Mother revived from her mysterious lethargy. On returning to life, one of her first thoughts was to ask for her Confessor. But the night was already advanced, and she was told that it was not a suitable hour to call him. She bowed her head, adored the designs of God, and placed herself in His hands to do in all things His adorable Will. In that moment she understood, by Divine light, that she must suffer without human aid, and that Our Lord would Himself strengthen her. She willingly accepted this additional trouble, and waited for the new assault which Hell was preparing for her. Her Confessor arrived early the next day, but the invalid was in such a condition that she could not understand anything. She became a prey to terrible convulsions, six persons being scarcely able to hold her. These violent attacks were caused by the frightful sight of the devils, and the unknown rigour of the tortures to which they would make her submit. But torments were as nothing to the heroic Elizabeth; every fresh torture caused her to hold the interior eyes of her soul fixed upon her God, from the fear of yielding to the diabolical suggestions which beset her. This extraordinary struggle betwixt the incomparable generosity of a woman, and the powers of darkness, armed with such violence and fury, endured for nine days and nine nights.

Her family, frightened by these extraordinary convulsions, called in a physician. He tried every remedy on his patient, but without result. The sufferings which Elizabeth experienced were too intense and of too strange an order to be subdued by human remedies. Thus his treatment had no effect, and she continued to be tortured in so frightful a manner, that those who were present were filled with horror and pity.

The physician understood that he was opposed by a supernatural illness, beyond all the resources of science. He said this openly to her Confessor, and counselled him to apply the remedies which his August ministry placed at his disposal. The Rev. Father Ferdinand of S. Louis knew this better than anyone else; he was not ignorant either of the nature or the cause of this terrible malady. Before she had become its prey Elizabeth had told him everything. He began to pray for his venerable penitent, and invited a great number of pious persons to interest themselves in trying to obtain a cessation of the illness.

Knowing that Elizabeth was suffering for the Church and for the Apostolic See, he conceived the idea of going to throw himself at the feet of the Sovereign Pontiff, and beg him to employ his all-powerful authority against the angels of Satan, who were raging with a bitter fury against the Venerable Mother. Pius VII. knew Elizabeth already, and how precious her life was to the Church in these times of extreme calamity.

On hearing the narrative of the terrible sufferings endured by her for the common cause of Christianity, the venerable Pontiff was greatly affected, and promised to use all the authority given him by his dignity as Vicar of Jesus Christ to repress the rage of Hell. His Holiness fulfilled his promise, and, what is worthy of remark, he foretold to the Rev. Father Ferdinand that the Venerable Mother would be freed on the day of the Purification of the Blessed Virgin; and this happened exactly as he had foretold. So many and such cruel torments had made the patient's body a real centre of pain. The boiling pitch poured into her eyes had blinded her, the sharp points which had torn her palate had contracted her mouth, in such a manner that she could not open it; her cheeks were burnt by two red-hot stones which the devils had applied to them; she felt in her neck such a violent pain, that it seemed that her head would be separated from her body, and all her limbs were contracted by the intolerable agony of the fire of Hell.

If her torments were horrible, the Divine favours which she received during the struggle were unequalled. Our Lord Himself strengthened her, tenderly calling her His beloved daughter; He filled her mind with ineffable light, and spread over her heart torrents of celestial joy in such abundance that she shed tears of happiness. But all these favours were surpassed by another. On seeing herself deprived of the Divine Eucharist, whose virtue makes martyrs, He gave her each day Holy Communion by the ministry of Angels.

One of the most frightful griefs which Elizabeth endured was that of interior desolation. She bore all other torments without a complaint; but, under the pressing desolation of this one, she could not help repeating with her adorable Saviour: "O my God! if it be possible, take from me this Chalice." But Our Lord consoled her, and encouraged her to offer herself to yet greater suffering for the Church and the Catholic Religion. When sorrow threatened to overwhelm her, He rejoiced her by casting upon her a ray of light, in whose midst she contemplated a consecrated Host. Each time that Our Lord spoke to her, the devils who tortured her precipitately took to flight, and Divine consolations filled and consoled her.

At length the great day of the Purification of Our Lady, indicated by the holy and August Pontiff Pius VII as the time of her deliverance, dawned, and the prophecy of the Vicar of Jesus Christ was accomplished to its utmost extent, and in the midst of the most remarkable circumstances.

On the morning of the Feast, the Blessed Virgin appeared to the heroic patient, accompanied by a numerous choir of holy Virgins and Martyrs, and compassionately approached the bed where she lay half dead. She ordered one of these Virgins to touch her eyes; she obeyed, and at the touch Elizabeth recovered her sight. During this action, the Queen of Heaven said to her: "This is Thecla, my beloved daughter, who has given you your sight.

Esteem her greatly, because she has so well known how to imitate my virtues." She then ordered S. Sylvia to touch her body; this she did, and cured her in all her limbs. Elizabeth shed tears of joy, and knew not how to display her gratitude for such a favour. At length, to show how agreeable to her was her generosity in suffering, the Blessed Virgin blessed her with great kindness, and promised her her all-powerful protection during her life and at the hour of her death. Thus ended this terrible struggle; thus will one day end the struggle of every just soul, if she be faithful to her God.

So many graces threw Elizabeth into an ecstasy of happiness, which lasted until the Feast of S. John of Matha, the 8th of February. During these six days, Our Lord visited her several times, and filled her each time with fresh consolation. She was also honoured with a visit from the Blessed Virgin and S. Joseph. One day the Blessed Virgin presented to her her Divine Child, saying to her: "Receive in your arms the Blessed Fruit of my womb. Love Him, for He is worthy of being loved." Elizabeth, overjoyed, pressed the Infant-God to her heart, and the impression of love which she then received was so strong, that she believed she would die; but she was reserved for many other struggles.

CHAPTER X

Elizabeth takes the habit of the Third Order of Bare-footed Trinitarians.—Our Heavenly Father threatens the Church with great afflictions.—The Venerable Mother offers herself as a victim of expiation.—Our Lord strengthens and arms her again for the fight.—She submits to a varied and cruel martyrdom.—She is overwhelmed with extraordinary favours in recompense for her generosity.—She drives away the devils by extraordinary means, and obtains a decisive triumph over them.

THE great favours which Elizabeth had received did not allow her to delay obeying an interior voice, which pressed her to become a Tertiary of the Order of Bare-footed Trinitarians. She had been called to this vocation of perfection as far back as the year 1807. At this period, her Confessor said to her: "The graces which Our Lord has showered upon you, prove that He asks something very great from you. Beg of Him to show you what is His adorable Will." The Venerable Mother obeyed, and she obtained this reply in the interior of her heart: "I wish you to become a Bare-footed Trinitarian." But whether her Confessor did not understand the import of these words addressed to a married person already the mother of a family, or whether he judged it prudent to await new orders from Heaven, Elizabeth made no further attempt to obtain this favour. In 1819, however, the year of the great crisis which we have related, she received an express order to ask for the habit of the Tertiaries of the Order of the Bare-footed Trinitarians. Our Lord manifested to her His Will on the Feast of Pentecost, at the moment when she received the Divine Eucharist.

The Venerable Mother, in her humility, dared not manifest to her Confessor what had taken place, persuaded that, knowing her as he did to be without virtue, he would never consent to so great a favour. On the following Sunday, the Feast of the Most Holy Trinity, Our Lord again intimated to her His Will; from that time she feared to resist, and communicated her inspiration to the Rev. Father Ferdinand of S. Louis, amidst a deluge of tears. Her prudent Confessor consoled her by gentle words, and recommended her to pray whilst he wrote to the Rev. Father General. He wrote, and the

General replied by sending him all the necessary powers to receive the vows of his venerable penitent.

In the year 1820, the pious ceremony of her admission took place. Our Lord had revealed to her the name which she should take on entering the Religious Life; she should be called Jane Felicia of the Blessed Trinity. The name of Jane gave her for her patron S. John, the beloved disciple, and reminded her of the peculiar love which Our Lord had never ceased to show towards her; that of Felicia, which signifies happy, moved her heart to gratitude for so many graces received; and the name of the Holy Trinity showed her that she ought to devote herself entirely to the glory of the Father, the love of the Son, and to leave herself henceforth to be guided by the inspiration of the Holy Spirit. Elizabeth understood all the mysterious sense of her new names. As soon as she returned home from the holy ceremony, she said to her daughters: "Everything has been done in accordance with the grace of Our Lord, but henceforth I must correspond with it. Pray for me, my daughters, that I may not abuse His mercies."

But, soon after, the Venerable Mother had to pass through such terrible trials, that all the precautions which Our Lord took to strengthen her were not too much. We have seen her come out victorious from a bloody struggle, let us now consider her in one yet more fearful.

On the Feast of the Immaculate Conception, 1820, she was ravished in ecstasy. In this condition Our Lord appeared to her, His countenance full of anger. He revealed to her the sacrilegious intrigues of the impious, even in Rome, for the destruction of the Catholic Religion, and He signified to her that He should at length bring down upon the world a frightful punishment. "Do not beg Me," He said, "to suspend the effects of My justice; henceforth I will no longer consider the sacrifices offered by My privileged souls, and I will not lend an ear to their ardent prayers." At the same time, He ordered the Holy Apostles Peter and Paul, as well as His Angels, to carry away the Apostolic See from Rome.

It is impossible to express the grief felt by Elizabeth at the conclusion of this terrible vision. She ran to throw herself at the feet of her Confessor, manifesting to him everything, and asking of him, in a voice broken by sobs, what she should do. Her wise director, after maturely reflecting on the prohibition of prayer which God had made for the appeasing of His justice, understood that these words were only a startling manner of expressing the extent of His anger, and he ordered Elizabeth to pray humbly to the Most High that He would not deprive the city of Rome of the Apostolic See. She immediately obeyed, and prostrating herself before the Heavenly Father, she prayed for the Church and for sinners with extraordinary fervour. Uniting herself to Jesus Christ upon Calvary, she repeated His adorable words: "Father, forgive them, for they know not what they do." With this intention, she offered herself as a victim of expiation to His fearful justice. Whilst she was thus absorbed in prayer, and torrents of tears flowed from her eyes, Our Lord appeared to her, and said: "Blessed daughter of My Father, your prayer is extremely agreeable to Me. Your sacrifice, united to My merits, will appease the anger of Infinite Justice." He then told her she must be prepared to suffer horrible torments from the spirits of darkness, for her body and her senses would be tortured by the most frightful agony, and her mind tried by an agony something like His own. He finished by promising to aid her, and to surround her with His most precious favours. The Venerable Mother, thus fortified, offered herself without hesitation to endure all sorts of tortures for the love of Him; she then reminded Him of her own weakness, and conjured Him not to abandon her to the fury of her enemies.

Our Lord, pleased at these sentiments of humble distrust, reassured her, and said to her: "Have confidence in Me; I promise you, as your God, that you shall gain the victory." At these words. He furnished her with the holy arms necessary to fight against Hell; He communicated to her the gifts of strength and intelligence, so that she might surmount all her torments, and laugh to scorn all the artifices of the malicious spirits. Furthermore, He enlightened her interiorly so as to give to her a perfect knowledge of her own nothingness, and to place her above the attacks of self-love and vanity.

In the beginning of January, 1821, Elizabeth imparted all these communications to her youngest daughter, so that she might know, as on the first occasion, the course she should take with her. The infernal assault began on the 22nd of January, the day on which the Church commemorates the Feast of the Chair of S. Peter. The Venerable Mother was struck by such an illness, that she lost all power of motion, and the use of her senses; they believed her to be dead. The physicians declared that there was no hope of recovery; during eight entire days, she could not swallow a single drop of water, notwithstanding all the efforts of her daughters to enable her to do so. In the first moments of this frightful lethargy, the devils presented themselves to her; and, amidst a tempest of derision and insults, they showed her the instruments of the most cruel tortures. At this sight, the intrepid Elizabeth, full of confidence in God, exclaimed: "I can do all in Him Who strengtheneth me. For the greater glory of God!" In her heroic ardour, she not only fearlessly witnessed their cruel array, but she willingly consented to support the agony of the torments which threatened her.

The infernal spirits threw themselves upon her, and cruelly beat her with iron rods in such a manner that her bones were broken under their blows. She would certainly have succumbed to the violence of this excessive torment, if a ray of divine light had not healed all her limbs, and delivered her mind from mortal desolation. At the same time, Our Lord tenderly embraced her, and rendered her still more courageous. Then the devils passed around her neck a circle of iron, which bound it with so much violence, that, as we have said, during eight days, she could take nothing. In consequence of this privation, and through the thirst occasioned by her torments, her throat and mouth were covered with ulcers. The appearance of her throat was so revolting, that those who were present could not see it without shedding tears of compassion. The devils tortured her yet more by tearing these wounds open with sharp instruments, so as to enlarge and renew them. The Venerable Mother often felt that she should die of pain; but a celestial light again shone over her, cured her, filled her with joy, and caused her to wish for other torments.

These hellish executioners, being thus vanquished, now invented a fresh torture. They made a cross, and fastened her upon it, forcing nails into her feet and hands. The tortures which Elizabeth endured reduced her to agony, and these malicious spirits said to her, mockingly: "See with what money God pays you. Abjure the fidelity which you have sworn to Him; otherwise, by dint of torments, we shall kill you." The magnanimous Christian replied by renewing her act of offering to Our Lord, and protesting that nothing should detach her from Jesus Christ, her Saviour and her God. At the sight of this heroism, these furious spirits plunged a lance into her side. In their rage, they satiated themselves with the spectacle of her sufferings, and enjoyed great satisfaction from them.

Suddenly one of them exclaimed: "She yet wants the title for which we have reduced her to this condition." All applauded the new invention. They took a piece of wood, on which they wrote the following words: "This is a true disciple of Jesus of Nazareth," and they nailed it to her feet with great strokes of a hammer. The torture which she experienced caused her to faint away; but the luminous ray again shone upon her, and she was cured. These cruel spirits then procured for her another kind of torture. During several days and nights they thrust into her ears spikes of iron, which caused so much torture in her head and neck, that she felt as if she were every moment at the point of death.

At the same time they made an attack upon her maternal love. They took the form of ferocious animals, and pursued her daughters, as if to tear them to pieces. Elizabeth's grief was inconceivable; in her fright she took in her hands her Crucifix and a relic of the true Cross, and prayed Our Lord to protect them against their cruelty. To heighten their malice, one of these barbarous monsters took the appearance of her Confessor, and, during eight days, did not cease to heap reproaches upon her. He turned upon her with a furious countenance, called her a hypocrite, a woman full of impostures, and worthy of the most infamous death for not having followed his counsel. These reproaches threw the Venerable Mother into a state of ineffable anguish. The devil carried his fury even further: whilst she was a prey to agonising convulsions on the cross, he threw at her five burning stones, which struck her in five different places of her body, and opened five painful wounds. But, at last, seeing that she triumphed over all his malice and blows, he went away in a transport of rage, and disappeared for ever.

The victory was gained; and it seemed that the whole of heaven wished to take part in this brilliant triumph. When Elizabeth was reduced to the last agony of anguish on the cross, and she invoked Our Lord, He appeared to her, resplendent with glory, and surrounded by a multitude of Angels. He took her down from the cross with His Divine Hands, and, by anointing her wounds with a sweet liquid which flowed from His sacred side, He cured her. He ordered the Angels to intone the hymn of victory, and the celestial Spirits formed a concert of divine harmony. Our Lord then took His heroic servant, plunged her into a torrent of sweetness which flowed from His face, and gave her a foretaste of eternal happiness. During this terrible struggle the Venerable Mother received other favours of a sublime order. The Blessed Virgin appeared to her several times, surrounded by a numerous Choir of Virgins, and addressed to her words so sweet and tender, that they threw her into an ecstasy of happiness.

Another time, the adorable Saviour came to visit her, accompanied by an immense number of Angels and Saints. S. Peter, the Prince of the Apostles, S. Paul, the glorious doctor of nations, sang in her presence the praises of the Most High. During this ineffable harmony, Elizabeth was ravished in God, and honoured with visions of which human language cannot express the grandeur. She was raised to the knowledge of the adorable mystery of the Holy Trinity, and the joy which she experienced from the contemplation of this great mystery was such, that she would not have been able to support its excess, without the special aid of Divine Grace.

Our Divine Saviour then addressed to her the following words: "Your brave and generous sacrifice has done violence to my irritated Justice. For the present I suspend the merited chastisement, as I still wish to show mercy. The Church will not be dispersed, nor Rome deprived of the Apostolic See. I will reform My people and My Church. I will raise up zealous Priests, I will send My Spirit to renew the face of the earth, I will reform the Religious Orders by the aid of wise and holy Reformers; they shall possess all the spirit of My beloved son, Ignatius of Loyola. I will give to My Church a new and learned Pastor, holy, and filled with My Spirit; in his ardent zeal he will reform the Church."

At the same time He gave her to understand by His Divine light, that since she had consented to descend living into Hell for the love of Him, she should be resuscitated before night, by the recovery of her health and the power to attend to her household affairs. He added that she would receive the gifts of the Holy Spirit, so that she would be in a better state to understand the Divine perfections, to be yet more inflamed with the fire of Divine charity, and to have the power of conversing still more familiarly with the adorable Trinity. It was on the 15th of February, 1821, that this glorious victory put an end to Elizabeth's fight with the powers of darkness.

If Satan exercises such cruelties upon the servants of God who enjoy the special protection of Heaven, what will he do during eternity to the unfortunate victims whom Divine Justice shall have given up for ever to his malice and fury? Hell never acknowledges itself conquered; filled with pride and the author of falsehood, the devil still lays perfidious plots, whilst the generous soul holds it enchained beneath its feet. Satan, seeing that his victim had escaped him, and that he could do nothing against her, tried to capture her by treachery, and to throw her again into the perils from which she had triumphantly issued. He suggested to the family that Elizabeth had become subject to fits of madness, and that this was the cause of the strange convulsions which had made her such a hideous spectacle.

Believing that this was the truth, Elizabeth's brother prepared thick cords to bind and control her. But Our Lord came to her aid; He informed her of all that was passing, and told her that she must purify the house from the wicked spirits which infested it, and confine them in a place where they could do no harm. Elizabeth rose at once, took the holy water font, and went over the whole house, ringing a bell, reciting the Psalms, and sprinkling holy water. The devils fled away at her approach; but Our Lord revealed to her that these malicious spirits had been shut up by the Divine power in a small box which He pointed out to her, and that, in punishment of their vain pride, they were there, filled with confusion, mixed with the seed which the box contained. At the same time He told her to take the box and empty its whole contents into the fire.

Elizabeth obeyed; but, by an infernal artifice, the seeds, on falling into the fire, exploded with so much violence, that the noise resembled a discharge of musketry. At this fearful detonation the whole family were terrified, not knowing what had happened. Without giving any notice of his intention, Elizabeth's brother took the cords which he had prepared, ran to his sister, and bound her tightly, imagining that she was going to give a new proof of her madness. At the same time a female servant of great strength took her by the legs, and bound them so roughly, that they were heard to crack as if the bones were broken.

Elizabeth strongly protested that she had never been at all mad; they would not listen to her, and she was bound like a deranged person. Whilst they were treating her in this manner, her Confessor arrived; all the members of the family immediately surrounded him to persuade him that Elizabeth was mad, and that it was necessary to bleed her copiously without delay. Father Ferdinand, at other times so wise and prudent, became shaken, and added his orders to the determination of the family. But Elizabeth's firm and respectful reply disconcerted him, and obliged him to take more time for consideration. She told him "that she venerated him as a Religious, but that she had no confidence in him as a physician; that if he would do her the favour to wait until the next day, he would certainly see that she was not mad; that, for the rest, she did not believe that she was bound to obey him in this case, because he was not competent to decide."

The surgeon came with his lancets; but she begged him to wait until the following day, and to do nothing hastily in a matter where there was no danger. The doctor, astonished to hear a supposed mad person speak with so much serenity, wisdom, and good sense, willingly granted her prayer. The next day, to the general surprise, she arose quite cured; and God thus made it known that He was the author of the strange scenes which had occurred. It was also said that the devils who were thus shamefully driven away surpassed a thousand in number. Satan, confused by this complete defeat, withdrew for a time, and left the Venerable Mother to enjoy the peace which she had purchased by so many and such cruel struggles. But this did not comprise all the fruit of her great victory. S. Teresa said that a single person, heroically faithful to God, suffices to suspend the anger of Heaven and save the world; we shall now witness facts which prove the truth of this oracle of the great Reformer of Carmel.

Blessed Elizabeth as a young wife

Letter of Blessed Elizabeth to her Confessor

Blessed Elizabeth and her children

CHAPTER XI

Our Lord renews His promise to Elizabeth, which He had previously made, of protecting Rome and the Sovereign Pontiff. —Conspiracy against His Holiness Pius VII.—Elizabeth discovers to him in a miraculous manner the perfidy of his counsellors, and he decides to remain in Rome.—She goes to give thanks to Our Lord in the Church of S. John Lateran.—Our Lord gives her a magnificent reception on her return from her pilgrimage.—Ingratitude of the Roman people for so many graces received.

AFTER the struggle which we have described, Elizabeth humbly prayed to God to remember His merciful promises, and to assist the Church, the Sovereign Pontiff, the Clergy, and all Religious Orders. Our Divine Saviour, who had already heard her prayers, confirmed to her anew all the assurances which He had given her, and He concluded by saying to her: "You see, My beloved daughter, My love for you induces Me to consent to your wishes and desires. Are you now content? Do you desire a further proof of My love?"

At these tender words Elizabeth was confused, and sinking her breast at her own nothingness, protested that she only wished in all things to do His holy Will, and that, if she had offered herself to suffer, it was because she had believed that in doing so she had entered into His own views.

These humble sentiments touched the heart of Our Lord, and He added: "Your holy desires, dictated by Faith, Hope, and Charity, which I implanted in your heart on the day of your Baptism with a particular predilection, and the other virtues with which I have chosen to enrich you, have rendered yon most dear to Me. My daughter, you have conquered My Justice. Rejoice, for the grace you have prayed for is already in your hands. I suspend the punishment, and, for the present, I give place to My Mercy."

On hearing these words, Elizabeth knew not how to reply; she humbled herself yet more, and said to her God that she could see nothing in herself which merited these great favours. She asked His pardon for her little correspondence with so many graces. She protested that she would live and die entirely abandoned to His

Divine Will, and she humbly asked of Him the grace to do so.

The time for the accomplishment of these merciful promises was not long delayed. The revolutionary party acting in the city of Naples provoked a rising in that capital. The conspiracy extended its ramifications throughout Italy, and had influential partisans even in Rome. The rebels found accomplices amongst the counsellors of the Sovereign Pontiff; these astute men counselled Pius VII. to leave the Eternal City, and to retire to Civita Vecchia. They alleged, as their reason, that he ought to place his precious life in safety; but the true motive for their perfidious suggestion was that, in the absence of the Sovereign, they could bring about a revolution with greater success.

The Venerable Mother knew by revelation of this perfidious plot, and through it conceived a mortal sorrow. Not knowing how to forewarn the Sovereign Pontiff of the snare which his own counsellors were laying for him, she hastened to her Confessor, informed him of what was passing, and prayed him to go himself to the Quirinal and expose the odious plot. The Rev. Father Ferdinand shuddered on learning these machinations; but he gave Elizabeth to understand that, under these circumstances, a visit to the Palace would not be prudent, that it would cause sinister reports, and make public a design which it was most necessary to keep secret. He then ordered her to pray to God to enlighten His Vicar as to his peril, so that he himself might come to a decision which would tend to his safety.

Elizabeth lost not a moment; in the ardour of her zeal she prostrated herself before God, and asked Him to reveal directly to His Pontiff the designs of the wicked, since there were no human means of warning him. Our Lord heard her in a manner as unexpected as it was wonderful. She herself related to her confessor what took place on this occasion (one of the most memorable of her life) in the following manner: "Our Lord at once vouchsafed a favourable answer to my poor prayers. He immediately gave such an impulse to my spirit, that, in an instant, I felt I could penetrate into the Quirinal Palace. There I was permitted to speak in full freedom to the Holy Father, and to tell him all that the Spirit of Our Lord had dictated to me. I gave him all the reasons necessary to prove that he ought not to leave Rome. He instantly acted upon what my poor mind had made known to him. Notwithstanding all that his counsellors could say to him, and in spite of his own previous convictions, although the carriage which was to take him away was already prepared, he left the Council, saying that 'instead of starting, he would go and lie down to rest.' The Austrians were charged with the duty of repressing the rebellion in Naples, and this was the end of a revolution which had seemed likely to overturn everything."

On the 26th of February, the Venerable Mother called her youngest daughter, and told her that she had received an order to make a visit to the church of S. John Lateran, to thank God for having delivered Rome from the misfortunes which it had deserved; that she should take possession of it in the name of all Catholics, and that she had acquired the right to do this by the cruel sufferings which she had endured. Her daughter was extremely astonished at such a communication. The pilgrimage to the church of S. John Lateran seemed to her beyond the strength of her venerable mother, because she was so feeble, that a prolonged conversation sufficed to make her fall into a fainting fit. Her Confessor, on being consulted, was of the same opinion as Mary Lucina; but, accustomed to the sudden changes which his pious penitent had often experienced, he added: "Let us leave it to Our Lord; if it is His desire that Elizabeth should make this journey, He will give her strength." God Himself had appointed the 1st of March for the day of the pilgrimage. Early in the morning she was quite as feeble as ever. A Priest came to say Mass in the little Chapel of Jesus of Nazareth, and Elizabeth received Holy Communion. After she had been nourished with the Life-giving Bread, she found herself quite changed; she felt a secret and mysterious vigour penetrate through all her limbs, so that she was able to accomplish this long pilgrimage without any difficulty. She would have made it on foot, if her Confessor had not prevented her.

Arrived in the august Basilica of S. John Lateran, the Venerable Mother there heard Mass, and prayed according to the inspirations of Our Lord. She then went to the Oratory of the Sancta Scala, and climbed all the steps by degrees upon her knees, without being helped by any one. On her return she desired to pay a visit to S. Mary Major, for she did not think it right to forget, on this happy day, her through whose hands pass all graces. Those who accompanied her could not restrain their astonishment at seeing this woman, who only a short time previously had seemed almost dead, bear so much fatigue with such perfect ease.

On her return home she received a welcome which her humility was far from expecting. "Our Lord appeared to her, in the midst of a multitude of Heavenly Spirits, tenderly blessed her, and called her His daughter, and one obedient to all His wishes." He ordered His angels to honour her as the daughter of His predilection and the arbiter of His Heart. At these words the angels intoned a canticle to celebrate the Divine Mercies. The harmonious concert ended, Elizabeth, who had an exceeding affection for the holy souls in Purgatory, begged Our Lord to deliver a great number for the crowning of this beautiful feast. The Angels instantly left, and soon reappeared with an incredible number of souls, each accompanied by her Angel Guardian. In her presence they took their flight to Heaven.

Our Lord, before withdrawing Himself, gave Elizabeth a knowledge of the wants of His Church, and recommended them to her prayers. Encouraged by so many favours, she, in her turn, begged Him to remember her benefactors, and have mercy on them. He promised her this favour with great kindness, and then disappeared.

One day, during an ecstasy, S. John the Baptist conducted her into an august and mysterious temple. The Blessed Virgin laid the Infant Jesus upon an Altar, and began to pray for the Church, supplicating her Divine Son to suspend the rigours of His Justice, and not to disperse the Ministers of the Sanctuary. She reminded

Chapter XI

Him that she was His Mother, and that, as His Mother, she hoped to be heard.

The Infant Jesus replied: "My justice will no longer support so many abominations. You are My Mother, but you are also My creature!"

With the august Queen of Heaven a multitude of Religious, united with their holy Founders, had also implored mercy. But scarcely had they heard the words of the Divine Infant, than they fell on their knees and adored the impenetrable decrees of the Most High. Then all the holy Religious offered to Him the incense of the good works of their respective Orders. The Infant God then raised His Hand, blessed them, and with them His faithful servant. The exile of the Sovereign Pontiff and the dispersion of the College of Cardinals took place very soon after this vision.

Another time three Angels conducted Elizabeth into a subterranean place where, in secret and in darkness, the impious were plotting the ruin of the Church. She there saw also persons covered with a mask of hypocrisy, who, under the specious pretext of doing good, secretly favoured the designs of the agents of Hell. The Venerable Mother was penetrated by a feeling of horror in presence of a sight of which the idea would never have presented itself to her mind. To console her, Our Lord showed her the re-establishment of the Society of Jesus, through the intercession of S. Ignatius Loyola. She also saw a Father of the same Society, illustrious by his knowledge and virtue, who, in union with other Fathers, defended the rights of Holy Church, and many others who shed their blood for Jesus Christ.

Actuated only by her zeal for the Church, Elizabeth, in her humility, addressed ardent prayers to Our Lord to obtain a cessation of this persecution. At that moment the All-Powerful caused His Justice to shine forth, and exterminated these wretches in a manner so prompt and terrible, that during several days her mind was troubled. She felt throughout her whole body a most intense terror, and experienced for a long time an icy coldness which ran through all her limbs. The following vision made an impression upon her no less vivid.

The Church appeared to her standing before the throne of God, supplicating Him to spare her children, and especially the Priests, Secular and Regular. But the Most High refused to listen, and said to her: "Take the part of My Justice, and judge your own cause." At these words the Church took off all her ornaments, aided by three Angels, executioners of Divine Justice; reduced to this sad state, she became so weak that she could not support herself. Then Our Lord gave her a staff to support herself upon, and a veil to cover her head.

In her desolation she bitterly sobbed, and deplored the solitude in which her children had left her. Suddenly the Spirit of the Lord invested her with a bright and intense light, which, spreading itself in four different directions, accomplished great and wonderful things. In the mild rays of this glory, those who slumbered in error arose, and re-entered her bosom, surrounding her with homage and respect. The Church appeared more beautiful and resplendent than ever. Six of the principal Religious Orders appeared as so many firm and strong columns destined to sustain her.

But, before enjoying this triumph, she had to pass through evils so frightful, that Elizabeth's Confessor was terrified by them. Desirous to avert them, he ordered his heroic penitent to go to S. Mary Major and make an entire offering of herself, of all the benefits she had received, and of those which she was to receive, in union with the offering of Jesus Christ upon the Cross. Elizabeth piously hastened to obey; and at the moment when she offered herself to Our Lord, two Angels descended from Heaven, received her offering in two chalices which they gave to S. Felix of Valois and S. John of Matha, who presented them to the Blessed Virgin, and she presented them to the Holy Trinity. The two chalices were placed before the throne of the Most High, and there remained to appease His just anger.

Our Lord confided to her His secrets; she wept unceasingly at seeing Him prepared to discharge upon the world the weight of His anger. She would have wished to deliver men, at the price of

Chapter XI

all her blood, from the evils which threatened them. But her prudent Confessor told her not to oppose the designs of God, and to content herself with praying in conformity with His Holy Will. She did so, and Our Lord, showing that He was moved, said to her: "This is a prayer worthy of Me." One day, however, the ardour of her zeal caused her to forget this rule. Having seen that God was about to show forth His Justice, she flew in spirit to the foot of His Throne, and incessantly prayed that He would stop His avenging arm. At that moment the chastisement would have drawn down upon many the loss of both body and soul.

One day she could not see, without extreme pain, so many persons of all ages and of every condition attach themselves to the perverse maxims of the world, and without shame outrage the God of all Majesty. In the ardour of her zeal to remedy this grave disorder, she offered herself to God to suffer all sorts of torments at the hands of men, and all kinds of vexations from devils. The Heavenly Father accepted her offering, and gave her the power of binding the devil who perverted so many souls, and of enclosing him in the abyss with the aid of two Fathers of the Order of the Holy Trinity.

In consequence of this vision, she set aside the next two months for the practice of all sorts of austerities: taking the discipline, multiplying her fasts and her watchings, and remaining constant in prayer. But in proportion as she appeased the Divine Justice, the impious again irritated Him by new crimes. Our Lord appeared to her, and told her that He repented of having listened to her prayers. At the same time He displayed before her eyes the thunderbolts which were ready to fall upon the guilty. Filled with terror, she hastened to Our Lord, and reminded Him of the offering which she had made of herself with His consent and at His invitation. The adorable Saviour led her into the Garden of Gethsemane, and taught her by His example the manner in which she should prepare herself for rude struggles and horrible sufferings. He ended by saying that, if she were faithful, a great recompense in His glorious kingdom awaited her. But the heroic

Elizabeth was not consoled by this prospect. She saw that men would not reform themselves, that they would be lost irretrievably, and this thought overwhelmed her heart with grief. She would have willingly consented to descend into the most profound abyss of Hell if, at this price, she could have saved men and repaired the outrage done to God.

When she learnt the news of the return of Pius VII. from his exile in France, she began to pray to obtain for him a prosperous journey. Several times she saw him surrounded by ferocious animals; but two Angels, one on his right hand and the other on his left, accompanied him. He had already entered his capital, when she perceived him, still in the midst of these horrible beasts, defended by these two Angels who were in tears. Elizabeth having respectfully asked of them the cause of their tears, they cast a sorrowful look over Rome, and exclaimed: "Ah! unhappy city, ungrateful people; the Justice of God will overtake and punish you. An ungrateful people, indeed, if such ever existed! An insubordinate nation, who have continually revolted against the Pontiffs, their august and legitimate sovereigns! but a happy nation, which, amongst all its excesses, always finds some generous soul to sacrifice herself for it, and to rescue it, as it were, in spite of itself from the perils which threaten it."

CHAPTER XII

Our Lord prepares the Venerable Mother for interior trials by symbolical visions.—She sees her soul under the form of a sick sheep, and afterwards under that of a pilgrim.—The way of perfection is represented to her by various steep and tortuous paths.—S. Joseph comes to her aid.—Our Lord reassures her, and promises her final perseverance.

OUR Lord, in His Almighty power, works in a wonderful manner, and attains many ends by the same means. In making Elizabeth expiate the sins of the world, He purified her senses, and refined her as in a crucible of suffering and love. But to become worthy of the sublime throne which He had prepared for her in the home of eternal bliss, it was necessary that she should pass through the more trying path of interior trials.

Bodily pain is grievous, especially when it proceeds from a supernatural principle; but the tortures of the mind are much more so. When the body suffers, the soul feels, as it were, only the rebound; when sorrow attacks the soul, nothing can express its intensity.

Our Lord, in His mercy, had prepared Elizabeth for sensible pain by symbolical visions; He now had recourse to them so as to prepare her for interior trials. Elizabeth saw her soul under the form of a sick sheep, with a wound upon her forehead, and a place upon her back where there was no wool. At the sight of these sores, she exclaimed: "Heal my soul, O Lord, for I have sinned against Thee." At this cry Our Lord hastened to her, under the appearance of a kind shepherd; He cured her head with His saliva, and washed the wound with His Blood. He ordered her to kiss Him, to mark her fidelity to grace. And whilst He caressed her with His Hand, the wool which was wanting was renewed. The sheep thus cured appeared so beautiful, that the Divine Shepherd, in a transport of joy, took her in His arms, and made her repose in His bosom. He then promised to protect her from her enemies, and to watch over her safety until her death.

Another time she saw herself placed on a road where she

could not distinguish the track. The night was dark, and the obscurity complete; she was in all the anxiety of a traveller who, in the midst of a thick forest, no longer finds his way, and is at every moment running the risk of becoming the prey of wild beasts. At that moment a celestial voice was heard, which told Elizabeth to look up to Heaven; she obeyed, and raising her eyes, she perceived a glorious light, by which she could easily guide her steps.

Another day her soul appeared to her under the appearance of a pilgrim, with a staff in her hand, the feet naked, and the head uncovered. Our Lord also came, dressed as a pilgrim, and said: "My daughter, you must pass through this forest. I will be your guide, come and follow Me." The Venerable Mother, fearing that this was some diabolical illusion, hesitated to go. Our Lord said to her: "Follow Me; do not be afraid that yon will be deceived: I am the Way, the Truth, and the Life." At the same time He shot from His Heart a ray of light, which reassured her, and she began to follow Him resolutely. In a short time the adorable Saviour disappeared, leaving her only a very feeble ray of light as a guide.

In another vision she found herself upon an exceedingly steep and slippery path. The obscurity was such that she could not see where to place her foot. In her desolation she cried to Our Lord. He seemed not to hear her. Her terror became inexpressible. Our Lord reassured her, and her fears vanished; the darkness again surprised her, and her terror was such that she believed she should die. Our Lord again quieted her, and promised her that He would never abandon her.

Another time she was a victim to inexpressible distress of mind, which she patiently endured, in union with the agony of Jesus in the Garden of Gethsemani. But she suddenly found herself transported to the borders of a lake, which she was obliged to cross without aid from any one. Frightened by the danger, she invoked Our Lord, and thus strengthened, she threw herself into the lake, full of confidence in the Divine assistance. At this moment Our Lord appeared, and told her that He was satisfied

Chapter XII

with her good will, and He carried her over Himself upon a shining cloud. Our Lord again disappeared, and Elizabeth discovered that her enemies had set a snare for her. The fear of yielding made the blood freeze in her veins; but she invoked the Name of Jesus, and then heard a voice repeat these verses from the ninetieth Psalm: "The Angels shall carry you in their hands, so that you shall not dash your foot against a stone. You shall tread upon the asp and the basilisk, you shall trample under foot the lion and the dragon." At these divine words Elizabeth found herself freed from all fear, and her soul remained full of confidence in God.

The most terrible pain which a soul experiences in internal afflictions, consists in an extreme desire to be united to God, and the cruel belief that this union is impossible. Elizabeth, while going through the whole series of interior desolation, could not escape from this, the most sorrowful of all. Before presenting her with this new chalice, Our Lord prepared her by another symbolical vision.

She was transported in spirit to the shore of a lake, whose fœtid waters spread a death-giving odour around. She was ordered to cross this pestilential lake, and to go to the other side. This command filled her with fear; the glorious Patriarch S. Joseph came to her, and offered to carry her upon his shoulders, but on condition that she should hold herself there without any aid. Elizabeth understood that she should actively co-operate in the protection of S. Joseph. Believing herself incapable of doing so, she began to weep. This sorrow lasted for twelve days; after which, to her astonishment, she suddenly found herself on the other side of the lake. The joy which she felt was so great that she did not know how to express all her gratitude to S. Joseph.

This suffering had scarcely ceased, when she fell into another not less cruel. She saw herself suddenly placed in an immense desert, without any road or track, and with no means of guiding herself through it. In this perplexity she sighed and wept; her body was oppressed, and all her limbs became feeble and languishing. This torture lasted from the 19th to the 25th of March, the Feast of the Annunciation of the Blessed Virgin. On this day Our Lord had compassion on her, and transported her in spirit into a garden of delights. The joy which she there tasted was so vivifying and salutary, that her soul forgot every feeling of sadness, and her body recovered all its vigour.

The visions which we have described were only a foreshadowing of what was to happen. If the symbols were so frightful, what would the reality be? Elizabeth was overwhelmed by a grief more cruel even than death. She had lost the feeling of the presence of God; it seemed to her that she was abandoned for ever. The sorrow and grief which she experienced from this cause were so great, that she often fell into a fainting fit which lasted for hours. The sword which pierced her heart, and made her, as it were, live in a dying state, was the sight of her ingratitude to God. In this depth of sorrow her love increased, and became as a furnace. But this ardour, which ought, it would seem, to have filled her with joy, only caused her a new martyrdom. Carried away by the vehemence of her love, she threw herself upon the bosom of God, but still retaining the feeling of her unworthiness; she believed herself to be the most criminal of all creatures, worthy even to be trodden under foot by all the devils in Hell.

In the midst of this violent battle between love and humility, she experienced the anguish of one who is unceasingly dying and yet cannot die. She said: "I cannot myself explain this kind of torment. It seems to me that it may be compared to that which is felt by the poor souls in Purgatory, who are possessed by a vehement desire to be united to the only Good, and are repulsed by Divine Justice."

Once she thought herself condemned to a cruel exile far from God. In this isolation she saw herself such as she was in herself; that is to say, deprived of all merit, an absolute nothingness, insupportable to herself. At the sight of her inexpressible misery, it seemed to her that the earth, unwilling to support her, would open beneath her feet, that the air would not give her breath, and that the devil would precipitate her into the abyss of eternal flames. She would have wished to purify herself from everything which rendered her unworthy of God; she would willingly have precipitated herself into Hell, if she had believed that these horrible flames would have had the power to take away her stains. In her utter helplessness to procure what she desired, she wept, and sobbed and cried for mercy, imploring Our Lord to show her what she should do.

"Thou knowest very well, O my God," she exclaimed, "that I love no one but Thee. I seek Thee in my anguish everywhere, and I find Thee nowhere." Then suddenly feeling at the bottom of her heart a loving response from Him Who had thus concealed Himself so as to make her seek Him more ardently, she added: "Now I feel that all the time that I was deprived of Thy presence, Thou wert with me."

She then fell into a swoon of love, fearing to lose her God Who had become the sole life of her heart. She writes: "This is a martyrdom so distressing to the soul, that no words can express it." The devil too came, and by his hideous appearance increased the atrocity of this torment. She saw him prepare for her such an artful snare, that she thought she could not escape it. The fear of falling into some sin made her feel that she should die of anguish. In order that she should not become the victim of her enemy, she never ceased praying; but she no longer found in prayer, as formerly, dear and sweet delight, but only dryness and bitter desolation.

It was time for Our Lord to come to the aid of His servant, so as to rescue her, at least, for some time, from this intolerable martyrdom. During sixteen days, Elizabeth had been a prey to these ineffable tortures, when, after Holy Communion, Our Lord consoled her with a vision. He appeared to her, holding her near Him under the form of a sheep; a gold chain, interlaced with precious stones, was round her neck. "Rejoice," He said to her, "O My well beloved; banish your excessive fear. Do you not see that you are united to Me by an indissoluble chain? No, never shall your enemies succeed in separating you from Me. Live in peace, love Me faithfully. I shall know how to acknowledge your love in time and also in eternity." A torrent of consolation filled Elizabeth's soul in consequence of this vision; but this happiness was of short duration.

Three days after she saw herself again surrounded by the thick darkness, which robbed her of the sight of God. Formerly, in her desolation, she could only weep for her sins; her eyes seemed like two inexhaustible fountains of tears; now her heart was dry and insensible. Nothing moved her; neither the remembrance of her sins, nor meditation on the Passion of Jesus Christ. These frightful aridities lasted for fifteen, twenty, and even thirty days. In the last year of her life she had to support this martyrdom during five consecutive months. At last this mysterious torture arrived at a degree of intensity which no words can express.

She often experienced a few moments' respite; but the relief was so little felt, that she was scarcely conscious of it. She only felt that God was working in the depths of her soul some secret operation, of which He would give her no understanding. She adhered to Him magnanimously; but her soul and body suffered cruelly. Our Lord, however, sustained her, and gave her superhuman strength.

Notwithstanding the intense suffering which she endured, the accomplishment of the Divine Will was her sole delight; she was so happy to conform herself to the pleasure of her Beloved, that her sufferings were transformed into transports of joy. She successively passed from the most intense delight to the most frightful desolation, and from the most vivid light to the deepest darkness. She said that these alternations without an interval formed a torment known only to God, and that, without special aid from Heaven, no one could support it without dying.

The Venerable Mother used a very expressive comparison to describe the pain of a soul exposed to the danger of losing her God. She compared it to a traveller who carries a treasure which he cannot conceal, on a road infested by thieves. "This treasure," she said, "is God; the soul cannot conceal it from the view of His enemies; she is obliged to carry it openly, exposed to all their attacks. There remains to her no resource but to invoke the aid of the Most High." She appeared to herself under the form of a person bathed in a cold perspiration. She saw her soul swiftly advancing, having her eyes constantly fixed upon her treasure, for fear that the enemy should suddenly come and snatch it from her.

Our Lord showed her how agreeable to Him was the care that she took to remain faithful to Him. He permitted her to see her soul already arrived in the harbour of salvation, and told her that there remained very little of the road to traverse before this would become a reality. The Angels accompanied her and encouraged her, and protected her against the attacks of her enemies. At last God Himself hastened to meet her, took her lovingly in His arms, and showered upon her the delight which flows eternally from His bosom.

CHAPTER XIII

Picture of the various symbolical visions which announced to Elizabeth the graces, gifts, and particular privileges with which Our Lord desired to surround her.—She contracts a celestial marriage with the Spirit of Love.—Our Lord plunges her into the bosom of inaccessible light.—S. Michael introduces her into glory.—She is chosen as the Spouse of the King of Glory.—She is confirmed in grace.—August ceremony of the mystical marriage.—She receives the glorious insignia of Queen for all eternity.—Wound of love; crucifixion and mystical death.—The Venerable Mother in a state of almost constant ecstasy.

THE object of the trials through which Our Lord caused Elizabeth to pass, besides the salvation of the Church and the Sovereign Pontiff, was to prepare her to receive the greatest favours. One day, after Holy Communion, she saw herself in spirit transported to a place of delight, enlightened by a sun of wonderful brilliancy. In the centre of this sun she perceived an eye which attracted her towards it. Three Angels accompanied her to this light, and she was immersed in it. As she advanced into this ocean of light she discovered a magnificent building in which resided the eternal God. Infinite Love gathered her to His bosom, and united her to Himself.

Another time she was ravished in a high place, which was inundated by a light of which that of the sun was darkness in comparison. She understood that Our Lord was communicating to her the knowledge of the mysteries of His Divine Perfections.

After another Communion, some Angels took her, and carried her away to a place where she enjoyed the most pure happiness. On her arrival, she found there certain celestial personages, who congratulated her upon the gifts which she had received, and gave great praises to God. God Himself kindly opened His arms, and invited her to come and throw herself upon His bosom. The servant of God, imbued with the feeling of her own nothingness, humbled herself, and attributed to Him the glory of all that there could be of good in her.

In 1809, the Divine Precursor appeared to her on the Eve of his Feast, and showing her the Promised Land, said to her: "Look!

there the Divine Paraclete awaits you, to celebrate with you celestial espousals. I will be your guide and conductor. O fortunate soul, what a happy fate is yours!" At these words, the Angels introduced her into the kingdom of Glory, and the Saint pointed out to her the Heavenly Palace, and began to describe its magnificence. Then he added: "But the door of this Palace is narrow: those who enter must be humble and lowly." Elizabeth immediately asked humility from Our Lord. She felt her heart renewed, so that she had the happiness of being able to enter.

One day, on a Feast of S. Ignatius Loyola, one of her chosen patrons, she saw her soul under the form of a dove, purifying itself in the merits of Our Lord, represented as a fountain of living water. Then a ray of light struck her, and seemed to cause her death, but a breath of wind restored her to life, and transformed her almost into a Seraph of love. Thus prepared, she entered into the Tabernacle of the Most High in the costume of a bare-footed Trinitarian. S. Ignatius and the Angels accompanied her, and the Patriarchs of the Order of the Blessed Trinity received her in company with many other Saints. There she received a mantle of inexpressible richness. When she was clothed with it, the Most High looked at her with great satisfaction, united her closely with Himself, and filled her with purity, holiness, and ineffable love.

On the 29th of September, the Archangel S. Michael appeared to her at the head of a numerous troop of Angels, and led her before the nuptial couch of the mystic Solomon. There she was plunged in an abyss of light, where she remained deprived of feeling; when she returned to herself, she heard the Angels singing the following verse of Psalm xxiii.: "Who will go up to the mountain of the Lord?" and they continued the psalm to the end. The divine harmony being ended, Our Lord promised to hear her prayers, and to bless those who had done her good, or who should do so in the future.

One day, when she was adoring the Blessed Sacrament exposed, Our Divine Lord appeared in the midst of a numerous body of angelic Spirits: His vesture of a purple colour, signifying

His ardent charity, and the amplitude of His precious mantle the greatness of His mercy. He held in His Hand a sceptre, ornamented with two figures, of which one was the emblem of justice, the other of mercy. In this majestic attitude Our Lord invested His beloved with a dress of extreme whiteness, sprinkled with precious stones, and gave her the gift of angelic purity. The God of love desired, by all these rich presents, to make her understand that He had chosen to raise her to the incomparable dignity of companion and Spouse.

Amidst so many extraordinary favours, Elizabeth never lost sight of her own nothingness; her humility was unalterable. One day she even went to Our Lord to beg Him not to introduce her into this mystical dwelling where He was accustomed to communicate Himself to the souls of His predilection, because she was not worthy, and to reserve such precious graces for other souls more faithful. This humble opinion of herself pleased Our Lord so much, that He instantly introduced her into the most secret places of His love. The effects which these sublime operations produced in Elizabeth were admirable. She rapidly traversed all the degrees of divine union, and arrived at last at an entire transformation of herself, which is the highest point. Her mind fixed always on God, nothing altered the peace of her soul; in all events, prosperous or unhappy, she adored the designs of Providence.

The knowledge which she had acquired in these miraculous communications penetrated the depths of heaven and earth. No created being was unknown to her. Among all the works which Our Lord had produced for His pleasure, by His power and His wisdom, one alone had presented to her mind an unfathomable abyss; this was the mystery of the Incarnation of the Word. She said that, as regarded this miracle, God had reserved the secret, and that even angelic intelligences would never know all its sublimity. When she came out of these ravishing visions, she seemed transfigured; and no one could be surprised, when so many gifts and graces had been bestowed upon her.

During a certain Easter Festival, Our Lord appeared to her with His Blessed Mother. He was so resplendent with glory, that Elizabeth remained entranced. The Divine Saviour invited her to come to Him, and told her that He was pleased to unite her to Himself, and to assist her by an entire transformation. At the same moment the servant of God saw herself like a white cloud inundated with light, and penetrated with glory by the Sun of Justice. Plunged in this ocean of inaccessible light, she felt that there were communicated to her, or, as it were, infused into her, the virtues of simplicity, purity, patience, sweetness, horror of the world, a desire to please God alone, and an extreme ardour to suffer for His Love.

God does not bestow such great favours except upon the elect; it is not, therefore, astonishing that He granted to the Venerable Mother a great privilege on the 2nd of July, the Feast of the Visitation of the Blessed Virgin, who appeared to her, and conducted her into Glory, so that she might contemplate the Throne of the Divinity. Whilst the humble Elizabeth prostrated herself before God to give Him thanks for so many favours received, Our Lord crowned her happiness by saying to her: "To-day you are confirmed in grace. You owe this remarkable favour to the powerful protection of this august Mother."

On Christmas night, Elizabeth had another vision which confirmed to her the same privilege. The Divine Child appeared to her holding in His Hand the heart of His well-beloved, with the Name of Jesus engraved upon it. He showed it to her, and said: "Be satisfied, you will love Me, you will love Me for ever. I have engraved My Name on your heart, and you can never forget it."

One day, on the Feast of S. John the Baptist, Our Lord asked her how much she loved Him. She replied: "O God of love, certainly I love Thee more than myself; and to prove my love, I am ready to give my blood and my life, and even a thousand lives, if I had them." Our Lord, pleased with this generous offering, replied to her: "You are indeed My well-beloved daughter."

Another day He made her a gift of special merits as a

Chapter XIII

privileged soul, and assured her that, by virtue of these merits, He would raise her to the rank of His Beloved Spouse. Eight days after, He crucified in her five inclinations of her own will, so as to enable her to fathom the Divine Perfections, to burn with love, and prepare her for the mystic nuptials.

This solemn preparation was made on the 24th of June, 1816. The celestial union which, for want of another name, says S. Teresa, is called a mystical marriage, took place only in the month of October in the same year. On the 19th, the Feast of S. Peter of Alcantara, Elizabeth was going to Holy Communion, when she heard a voice, which said to her: "On the 23rd Our Lord will contract with you a sacred marriage. This favour which I bestow upon you equals that which I was pleased to grant to my worthy servant Catherine of Sienna."

The humble Elizabeth, on hearing these words, was troubled, and calling to mind the sins of her whole life, she began to weep bitterly over them. Our Lord came to her aid, and again enriched her with the gifts of humility, contrition, and love. At length, the 22nd of October having passed, Elizabeth determined to pass the night in prayer and praise, until the next morning, the day appointed by the celestial voice.

It seemed as if Our Lord had hastened to give to His beloved this supreme mark of His Love. Midnight had scarcely struck when the room was illuminated. The Blessed Virgin appeared, carrying in her arms the Blessed Infant. The Divine Child called Elizabeth, and told her to come to Mary, the Throne of His mercies. At this sight, Elizabeth was so confused that she desired to conceal herself. She approached them, trembling. Then the Divine Infant placed on her finger a precious ring, and communicated to her so much love that she seemed to be in the midst of an immense fire. He then gave her a new heart, like His own, and purified her in a miraculous water which poured forth from His sacred side.

This ceremony was accomplished in the presence of a numerous company, who shared in the happiness of the new Spouse of the King of Glory. Elizabeth received the congratulations of the Queen of Heaven, who on this occasion held the office of Bridesmaid; of S. Joseph, her chaste and virginal Spouse; of the Three Kings, of the Patriarchs of the Order of the Most Blessed Trinity, and a multitude of angelic Spirits. The delight which the Venerable Mother experienced during this night made her beside herself, and during fifteen days she fell into continual ecstasies.

In 1822, on the Feast of the Most Blessed Trinity, Our Lord vouchsafed to renew the same favour to His servant, but with more majestic surroundings. He began by profusely infusing into her soul the gifts of Faith, Hope, and Charity, and all moral virtues. He then placed her in a fire of love, where she was purified from the slightest stains. After she had been thus prepared by the Divine Mercy, the celestial Spouse ordered His Angels to give to His beloved precious garments suited to her august dignity. She immediately saw the celestial Spirits place upon her right arm a symbolical maniple, bind her loins with a sacred cord, place upon her left arm an inpenetrable shield, and cover her entirely from head to foot with a long veil of incomparable whiteness.

At the same time, she understood the signification of these various ornaments. The maniple was the mark of a lively faith, filled with good works; the buckler was the emblem of a firm and unshaken hope; the cord was the emblem of angelic chastity; and the two tassels which hung from the extremities and descended to the ground were the sign of deep humility. The veil which was thrown over all the other ornaments indicated a royal charity which enhances the value of all other virtues.

When the Venerable Mother was thus clothed, as it had pleased God to command, He invited her to the eternal nuptials. This appeal made by the Almighty caused a glorious transformation, which gave to Elizabeth the grandeur and majesty of an incomparable Queen. A ray of glory shone over her whole person, and gave her a more resplendent dress; she saw a powerful sceptre in her left hand, and a staff of command in her right, and her forehead was encircled by a crown. She understood that these new emblems signified the different degrees of glory which

Chapter XIII

awaited her in the mansions of the Blessed.

On seeing such gratuitous liberality on the part of God, she began to weep for her sins in such a manner that Our Lord had pity on her. He consoled her by telling her that her lowliness and poverty were doubtless very great, but that the ardour of her love had wiped away all the rest.

The more this privileged soul drew near her end, the more the God of love increased in her the devouring flames which consumed her. He desired to make her a terrestrial Seraph, who might indemnify Him, by the intensity of her charity, for the guilty coldness of the world, and He spared nothing to raise her to the summit of love. He had already repeatedly pierced her heart with burning arrows, which had detached her from all creatures, and placed her above all human affection; but in the year 1823, on the Feast of the Visitation, he gave her, as we may say, the last crowning gift of grace. This occurred two years before her death.

The Venerable Mother had just received Holy Communion when Our Lord, suddenly showing Himself to her, took from His divine quiver an extremely sharp and precious arrow, and buried it deeply in her heart. This burning weapon inflamed Elizabeth with so much ardour, that she did not know how to express or contain herself. The effects of this divine wound were ineffable. When her spiritual Father commanded her to describe it, she replied that human language had no words to give expression to such profound mysteries.

Another day Our Lord showed her a Cross, saying to her: "My love will crucify you upon this Cross." This prediction was verified on a Friday in March. She was transported in spirit to Calvary, where she perceived three Angels with a Cross, a hammer, nails, and a crown of thorns. The Angels invited her to lie down upon the instrument of execution; she immediately did so, with great respect and profound modesty. Then they forced the mysterious nails into her feet and hands; it seemed that she would suffer great torture, but she experienced only delight and ineffable transports of love. Then they placed the crown of thorns upon her head, and instead of cruel pricks, this holy diadem communicated to her a miraculous light regarding the mysteries of our holy Religion, and particularly the august mystery of the Most Holy Trinity.

Our Lord then appeared to her under the form of a beautiful and gracious young man, looking kindly at her, and then, in a transport of love, he plunged a dart into her heart. The Blessed Virgin, who was present at this divine scene, approached her, and embraced the Cross.

Once, on a Good Friday, Our Lord honoured her with another crucifixion yet more sweet and touching. She went to visit a sepulchre, when she was suddenly ravished in ecstasy, and transported to the summit of a mountain. There she saw a Cross and the other instruments of the Passion radiant with glory. Some Angels were at the foot of the Cross, and adored it, whilst plunged in grief and sorrow. She fell upon her knees, and also adored the glorious instruments of our salvation. In that moment she felt herself penetrated by such a lively sorrow for her sins, that she fell down breathless, and seemed to be dying.

Our Lord then ordered His Angels to carry her to the top of another mountain. When she arrived there the adorable Saviour surrounded her with a bright light, and contracted with her an ineffable union. At the same time he said: "Come, and unite your heart to mine." Scarcely were these words pronounced, when Jesus showed Himself, holding in His hand a Cross and the other instruments of the Passion. He told His beloved to lie down upon the nuptial bed; she obeyed, and our Divine Saviour crucified her Himself.

He then took a sword with two edges, plunged it into His adorable side, and then drawing it out, all empurpled with His precious Blood, He thrust it into her side. This wound and this mixture of the precious Blood of Jesus with Elizabeth's blood placed the seal on a union of which the perfection was known only to God.

On the same day, at three o'clock in the evening, Elizabeth was meditating on the Agony of the Divine Saviour. The ecstasy returned, and she was transported to Calvary, where she was an eye-witness of the Man-God. She saw her Divine Redeemer insulted, and overwhelmed with outrages by a multitude of His enemies. Then a portion of these wretched people recognised their error, repented, and struck their breasts as a sign of sorrow. She also began to deplore her sins amidst a torrent of tears.

Our Lord told her to pray, and to offer her merits to the Heavenly Father for the conversion of seven sinners, whose salvation He desired. Elizabeth immediately obeyed. As soon as she began to pray she felt the most frightful pains in her hands and feet, particularly in her left foot, and the whole of the left side as far as the shoulder. She offered all these sufferings in union with the merits of the Divine Crucified, for the sinners whom He had recommended to her.

Our Lord then told her to take a golden hook which He had placed in her heart, to throw it into the mouth of the seven sinners, and to bring them to Him by a golden chain attached to the hook. She executed this order with the aid of three Angels who were sent to accompany and help her. These unhappy creatures, being drawn to the foot of the Cross, vomited an infectious matter, and shed a great quantity of blood. The hooks fell of themselves, but each was found multiplied by seven. She took them and plunged them into their hearts. At the same moment these men changed their appearance, from being frightful beasts as formerly, they became tender and graceful lambs. But as their colour did not satisfy the Mother of God, she sent forth from her merciful bosom a ray of light, which, falling upon them, rendered them whiter than snow. On seeing so many wonderful things, Elizabeth intoned a canticle of thanksgiving.

It often happened to the Venerable Mother to participate in the sorrows of her crucified Love. Once on a Good Friday she was ravished in spirit upon Calvary, and there was a witness of the Crucifixion of the Man-God. The compassion which she experienced caused her to feel the torments of her adorable Saviour to such a degree that her weakness could not support such an excess of pain; she fainted away, fell upon the ground, and remained there three hours as if deprived of life.

One Friday in Lent Our Lord invited her, after Holy Communion, to accompany Him to Calvary. The sufferings which she experienced during four hours and a half were extreme. On the night of the second Friday in Lent she participated in the anguish of the Agony of Jesus in the Garden of Gethsemani, and in the atrocious sufferings which he endured in climbing Calvary. These torments were so frightful that, as she herself acknowledged, she would have sunk without miraculous aid.

But, as soon as she was in danger of death, Our Lord strengthened her mind, and healed her body; He also gave her sublime instructions, and inflamed her with a new desire to imitate His example and, above all, His sufferings.

On another Good Friday Our Lord gave her to understand what was His design in overwhelming her with so many privileges and graces. Transported in spirit to Jesus agonising, she experienced an ardent desire to suffer. To satisfy her, Our Lord sent His Angels, who nailed her to the Cross in the presence of Jesus Himself. The adorable Saviour, desiring to crown this remarkable favour with His own hand, shot into her heart a dart of love which gave her a mystical death.

In this state she saw her spiritual Father, who received an order to transport her thus crucified to a high mountain, and to learn from him the Will of God. Elizabeth heard all with the most profound respect, and promised to obey the voice of Our Lord. At the same moment the whole mountain was covered with souls of the elect, who proposed to imitate her example and to invest themselves in the Third Order of Trinitarians. Our Lord had several times given her to understand that He wished through her to give new impetus to this Order, formerly so celebrated, and now so little known.

Every day the Venerable Mother made the Way of the Cross; during this Office she wept bitterly for her sins. It then seemed to her that all imaginable torments were not capable of expiating what she called her perfidies. One day she exclaimed: "Lord, what did You do whilst I was wandering far from Your love? Had You abandoned me to my malice only to give me up afterwards to the rigours of Your justice?" Our Lord appeared to her, and replied: "No, My daughter, no. In that moment I was pleading your cause with My Father with as much ardour as if My happiness had depended upon the possession of your heart."

It was meditation on the sufferings of Jesus which rendered her capable of enduring all the punishments of hell. The most cruel torments could scarcely appease her hunger for suffering: she continually asked for new ones. Our Lord one day said to her: "Oh! what pleasure you cause Me, dear daughter! I shall know how to reward your love."

All these favours so often repeated, and the operations of grace in her soul, raised Elizabeth, as it were, to a condition of continual ecstasy. At every moment she was beside herself, immovable; ecstasy and ravishment surprised her everywhere, in the Church, in her oratory, at table, during work, whilst at prayer, at Holy Communion, and even in the midst of a conversation.

CHAPTER XIV

Detailed recital of various apparitions made to the Venerable Mother.—Apparition of the Infant Jesus, of Jesus in the Cenacle, of Jesus suffering.—Apparition of the Blessed Virgin under different forms and in many of her mysteries.—Devotional practices by which Elizabeth prepared herself for the Feasts of the Blessed Mother.—S. Peter and S. Paul appear to her in a symbolical vision which relates to our times.—Apparition of a great number of other Saints.

THE life of Elizabeth had become, as it were, a continual chain of visions and revelations. Our Lord had chosen her to be a powerful mediatrix; this elevated mission required almost continual communications between heaven and earth. The mystery which the Venerable Mother could not withdraw herself from contemplating was that of Jesus in the Crib. So that she might be more influenced by the moving spectacle of a God born in poverty, under the half-ruined roof of a miserable stable, she always erected a little crib at Christmas in her oratory. Elizabeth made this place the object of her delight, and could not leave it without sorrow. It often happened that she knelt down there at the beginning of the night, and forgot the lapse of time in contemplation, so that only with the first light of the sun, on the following day, she arose from her ecstasy.

She received in this privileged place graces of the highest order. She told her youngest daughter that Our Lord often ravished her in spirit, and led her to the adorable grotto in Bethlehem. One day, being penetrated with the fear that she did not faithfully co-operate with the favours of God, she asked of Him the gift of perfect correspondence. The Infant God appeared to her, gave her a small cross, and said to her: "Take! O My beloved! take this little cross: it will assure you of the grace which I have communicated to you." He thus made her understand that the most efficacious means of ensuring fidelity to heavenly graces, is to embrace suffering generously.

Another time she prayed for the Church and its Ministers. At that moment the Infant God showed Himself lying in His crib, and bathed in His Blood. At this sight Elizabeth believed that she should die of grief, and asked who had had the barbarity to reduce Him to such a pitiable condition. The Divine Infant replied: "This is done by those very Ministers for whom you are praying: the monks and nuns who profane their holy habit; the fathers and mothers, who, instead of giving their children a Christian education, inspire them with a love of pleasure and luxury, and fill them, from their earliest childhood, with worldly ideas."

Three Angels presented themselves before the just God, to draw down His vengeance for these crimes; but the Blessed Virgin hastened and prayed her adorable Son to suspend the dreadful consequences of His anger. Then the Divine Child raised His hand, and said to them: "Stop! stop!"

During the Feast of the Purification, the Blessed Virgin showed her the Divine Infant streaming with blood, and said to her: "See, my daughter, how He is wounded! hide Him in your heart." Elizabeth promptly obeyed. On the next day the Queen of Heaven commanded her to offer to the Heavenly Father the precious Blood of His adorable Son, together with her own sorrows and her ardent love, to obtain the salvation of the souls whom she protected. The Venerable Mother prayed for a long time with the fervour of a Seraph; but she could never know whether her prayers were accepted or rejected, so much did the crimes of men weigh down the balance of Divine Justice.

However, the love which Our Lord lavished upon her knew, as it were, no limits. One night when she was in prayer she was transported in spirit into the supper-room in Jerusalem, and had the happiness to assist at the Last Supper. She saw our Divine Saviour consecrate the Bread and Wine, and distribute both to His disciples. In her humility she dreaded to present herself at this august banquet; but Our Lord called her and gave her with His own Hands the Divine Eucharist. Elizabeth, supremely happy, then fell into a loving sleep, and, like S. John, reposed on the adorable breast of her Divine Master.

Our Divine Saviour treated her as a confidante and friend. On one Thursday of the Carnival, at the moment when she was receiving Holy Communion, she saw Him all covered with wounds, and heard Him say to her: "Come, My beloved, come and console My Heart." Elizabeth, who had always the thought of her sins present to her mind, exclaimed: "Ah, Jesus! I know well: they are my sins which have reduced You to this condition." Our Divine Saviour replied: "You may dry your tears, O My beloved daughter. Come and make amends for the injuries which I receive from those who give themselves up to guilty pleasures."

After another communion Our Lord showed her three souls, who, under the form of sharp thorns, pierced His heart. The sorrow which she experienced at the sight of this heart-breaking spectacle was extreme. She would have snatched away these thorns at the price of all their torments. Suddenly three Angels, each bearing a chalice, presented themselves before her. The first gave her an instrument with which to draw out the bloody thorns, and told her to put them in his chalice. The second offered her in his chalice a precious balm, and put in her hands an instrument with which she could cleanse the wounds and anoint them so as to heal them. The third had his chalice covered; he uncovered it, and Elizabeth saw three precious stones shining in it. At the same time she heard the following words: "Take these precious pearls, O My beloved daughter, and come and adorn My Heart with them."

Elizabeth took them, and made some ornaments with them for the adorable Heart of Jesus. She had scarcely finished, when our Divine Saviour, to recompense her, shot from His sacred Person three rays of fire, which penetrated her soul, and united her closely to Him Who is all love. He also told her that the precious balm which had served to anoint His wounds, were the tears which she had shed to indemnify Him for the offences committed against Him by these three guilty souls. Elizabeth had several times visions of the same kind, after Holy Communion, with this peculiarity, that Our Lord appeared to her under the form of a beautiful and graceful Infant.

The Venerable Mother lived in an intimate and filial

connection with the Queen of Heaven. In 1815, on the day of the Immaculate Conception, she saw her descend from heaven, in the Choir of the Trinitarian Religious, amidst a great number of Angels, the holy Founders of the Order, and many of their disciples. The Mother of God showed a particular tenderness for the Father who directed her, and for two others already deceased. She presented to them a cup filled with a precious liquid, saying to them: "Take this, my children; this will preserve you from all hurtful influence." These words were in allusion to the peculiar dangers to which these Fathers were exposed whilst the soldiers occupied their monastery, and from which they had been delivered by a special protection of Heaven.

The holy Founders of the Order then prayed the Queen of Heaven to allow Elizabeth also to drink from her cup. She did so, and in presenting it to her, she said: "This will render you strong in suffering, constant in danger, and tranquil at the hour of death."

The following vision was accompanied by a peculiar privilege, and is consoling to married persons if, amid the dangers of their state, they preserve themselves pure and chaste. Elizabeth prepared herself with great fervour to celebrate the Feast of the Assumption of the Blessed Virgin. S. Ignatius Loyola appeared to her, and advised her to prepare herself to be crowned by the Hand of Our Lord. The adorable Saviour soon appeared, dressed in a splendid robe, marked with the Cross of the Trinitarians, and placed upon her head a rich diadem. The Archangel S. Michael, at the head of a legion of angelic Spirits, assisted at this august ceremony, as well as S. Ignatius and the holy Founders of the Trinitarian Order. When she was thus adorned with the insignia of royalty, Our Lord conducted her before the throne of His Blessed Mother, and made her enrol herself among the Virgins who composed her Court. Elizabeth was made so happy by this unexpected favour, that she remained in ecstasy during three consecutive days.

On another Feast of the Assumption, this inappreciable favour was solemnly confirmed to her. She saw herself suddenly

Chapter XIV

transported before the throne of the Queen of Heaven, in order to offer her her congratulations, and to pay her the most profound homage, amidst the Angels and their glorious chiefs, the holy Apostles, and a great number of Virgins. Humbly prostrate before the incomparable Sovereign of Angels and of men, she told her that she had an ardent desire to honour her, and that for the love of her, she would willingly give a thousand lives if she possessed them.

The gracious Queen cast upon her a look of pleasure, and said to her: "Come to me, beloved daughter, fear nothing; I will inscribe your name amongst those of my beloved daughters." At the same moment the Virgins of Heaven joyfully opened their ranks, and received her into the number of those happy privileged souls.

Another Feast of the Assumption was the occasion of her receiving a favour yet more solemn. Ravished in spirit into the realms of Glory, Elizabeth contemplated the Blessed Virgin seated in her majesty upon a throne of incomparable grandeur. Three ranks of Virgins composed her Court. The first rank were adorned with diadems upon their heads, the second wore suspended from their necks and hanging on their breasts celestial arms, the third held in their hands bouquets of flowers.

The Archangel S. Michael led Elizabeth to the foot of the throne. The august Queen placed a precious diadem upon her head, so as to make her worthy to take her place among the Virgins of the first rank. She then presented her to the Heavenly Father, Who received her with great kindness, and endowed her with an abundance of graces, for herself, for the living, and for the dead. The same vision was renewed during the last year of her life.

We may easily understand that after such precious favours, Elizabeth should become indefatigable, as it were, in showing to the Blessed Virgin her devotion and her love. Every day she recited, as a double tribute, the Rosary and the Little Office. She inculcated in her daughters the same habit, and they made these prayers together. She incessantly invoked her by ejaculatory prayers burning with love. On the Eves of her Feasts she fasted rigorously on bread and water. She sanctified the Novenas and Octaves by numberless mortifications and frequent penances. She then said with her daughters the following prayer: "I rejoice with you, O Blessed Virgin Mary, for the remarkable honour which Our Lord has bestowed upon you in this mystery" (for example, of the Assumption, the Annunciation, etc.). "I return most hearty thanks to the Blessed Trinity, and I unite my gratitude to that of the blessed souls in Paradise." She added five times the Gloria Patri, inclining her head each time, and then kissing the ground. She repeated this prayer ten times.

Elizabeth had also a tender devotion to S. Michael, and received great favours from him. On one of his Feasts she had the happiness to be transported in spirit into the regions of Glory. She saw the illustrious rank which he occupied near the throne of the Blessed Trinity, and she was a witness of the homage paid him by the whole host of Heaven. Once she perceived her Guardian Angel among the Heavenly Spirits. He surpassed all the others in beauty and in glory, for he was one of those whose place was nearest to the throne of the Divine Majesty.

She diligently applied herself to honour S. Joseph, the glorious Spouse of the Blessed Virgin, and S. John the Baptist, the Divine Precursor. She once made the exercises of the month of March to obtain from the illustrious Patriarch the virtues of humility, purity, singleness of intention, and love of God, and, in fine, all the graces necessary to imitate him, and to follow in his footsteps. In order to show to Elizabeth how agreeable this worship was to him, the glorious Saint sent to her an angelic embassy to invite her to the virginal nuptials with the Heavenly Spouse.

S. John the Baptist also appeared, resplendent with glory. He wore a rich mantle, embroidered with pearls and diamonds, which betokened his sublime virtues, more especially those of humility, purity, and charity. He conducted her himself before the throne of the Eternal, and taught her to humble herself in His presence for all the favours which she had received from Him.

One of the celestial personages who most frequently favoured her with his visits was S. Peter, Prince of the Apostles. One day he ordered her to cause a church at Albano, dedicated to him, which had fallen into ruins, to be restored. He mentioned to her the person who would supply the money necessary for this purpose. She had, indeed, only to present herself to the person indicated, when she obtained all that she desired.

The following vision produced a great sensation in the Holy City. On the Feast of S. Peter, Elizabeth prayed the Apostle to succour the Church whose guardianship had been confided to him, and to pray for the sinners who dishonoured her. Suddenly the heavens were opened, and the Apostle S. Peter descended, dressed in pontifical vestments, and surrounded by a numerous troop of angelic Spirits. With his pastoral staff he traced a large cross upon the ground: he touched its four extremities, and four mysterious trees, full of flowers and fruit, arose. Then he opened the doors of all the monasteries, both of men and women, and returned to heaven. The four mysterious trees were to serve as a place of refuge for all the faithful who had the happiness to preserve the sacred deposit of the Faith, during the cruel trial which Our Lord was about to send upon His Church.

At the same moment the heavens were covered with dark clouds, and such a violent wind was let loose, that both men and animals were filled with terror. In this horrible confusion, men devoured each other, the devils themselves mixed in the carnage to multiply the victims. But what was most remarkable, they could vent their homicidal rage only on the impious; the good, sheltered under the four mysterious trees, were in safety, under the protection of the holy Apostles SS. Peter and Paul.

When the Divine Justice was appeased, by the effusion of so much blood and the destruction of the impious, the clouds which obscured the heavens were dispersed, and a mild ray of light announced to the earth the reconciliation of God with men. The Apostle S. Paul appeared full of power and strength; he took the devils, loaded them with chains, and led them to the feet of the Prince of the Apostles. S. Peter held sovereign power to judge them: he condemned them to be precipitated into the abyss, and the sentence was immediately executed.

In order to celebrate this glorious victory, the Angels mingled with the Faithful who had not failed during the trial, and conducted them to the feet of S. Peter, who received their homage and thanks, seated upon a majestic throne. He himself chose the new Pontiff who was destined to reorganise the Church. The Religious Orders were re-established, the Faithful were inflamed with new fervour, the Church recovered her primitive beauty, and the Sovereign Pontiff was recognised in every country of the world as the Vicar of Jesus Christ.

This marvellous vision contained, under symbolical forms, the Apocalypse of our times. The servant of God might have added with the prophet of Patmos: "The time is at hand. He that hurteth, let him hurt still; and he that is filthy, let him be filthy still; and he that is just, let him be justified still; and he that is holy, let him be sanctified still. Behold, I come quickly; and my reward is with me, to render to every man according to his works."

The Prince of the Apostles condescended to give Elizabeth useful advice for the good of her soul. He assigned to her as her particular Director, the Apostle S. James the Great, who, indeed, zealously occupied himself with her spiritual progress. He showed her a narrow path, but straight and direct, which would conduct her rapidly to God; this was the way of interior and exterior mortification. He also urged her to put away all terrestrial affection; and, on these conditions, he promised her on the part of Our Lord a closer union to aid her in attaining a fresh degree of love. This union rendered her a participator in the Divine Justice. This new favour was granted her by the mediation also of S. Ignatius Loyola, S. John of Matha, and S. Felix of Valois.

Elizabeth had a great devotion to S. Ignatius Loyola. "I call him my Father," she said, "because he loves me as much as his own children; I call him my Master, because he has taught my soul divine science; I call him my Protector and my Advocate, because he had the kindness to obtain for me from the incomparable

Chapter XIV

Mother of God the celestial gift of divine charity."

S. Ignatius also presented her to S. Felix of Valois and S. John of Matha, and obtained for her the favour of daily Communion. She then said: "Oh! how many times I have offered to Our Lord my blood and my life, to obtain that His Congregation, the Company of Jesus, might be re-established."

The Saint revealed to her the particular love which Our Lord had for her, and how much she had still to do to conquer flesh and blood. He also exhorted her to place all her confidence in Our Lord, and said to her: "Fear nothing, O soul purchased with the Blood of Jesus Christ! You will be victorious over yourself and your enemies; you will rise to a most eminent degree of perfection."

The favours which she obtained by the intercession of the Saints of the Trinitarian Order were incalculable. On the Feast of S. John of Matha she was ravished in spirit during the holy sacrifice of the Mass, and being purified by a ray of light, she was invested with the holy habit of the Order. A multitude of Angels, and a great number of blessed souls who had belonged to this Order, came to her, and congratulated her upon such a great favour. To crown her joy, Our Lord revealed to the Angels and Saints who were present the designs which He wished to accomplish through her.

Seven days later the Blessed John Baptist of the Immaculate Conception, the author of the Reform of the Barefooted Trinitarians, appeared to her and said: "My daughter, do not refuse the favours of the Most High, but adore His divine judgments, and receive His grace with humility."

On the Feast of S. John of Matha, when she was going to receive Holy Communion, she saw this Saint come to her with S. Felix Valois. Whilst she communicated, they held before her a cloth of precious material, and two Angels who accompanied them, each held a lighted torch.

On the Feast of S. Felix of Valois she recommended herself to him to obtain the grace of suffering in union with Jesus crucified.

In order to give more weight to her humble prayer, she offered it by the mediation of S. Michael of the Saints, and of the Blessed Simon and John Baptist of the Immaculate Conception, all three Religious of the Trinitarian Order. All these holy persons appeared to her and conducted her to the throne of S. Felix of Valois. Elizabeth addressed her prayer to him, and conjured him to be favourable to her.

The glorious Patriarch extended his hand towards her, and placed it upon her head. Elizabeth received the order to renew her vows, and to renounce all sensible consolation. She obeyed. The Saint received her vows and her heroic renunciation under the form of precious stones, and, in union with the three Saints, he offered them to the Most High, who deigned to accept them. In return for this generous act Our Saviour contracted with her a new degree of union, and favoured her with the precious gift of His divine love.

On the following day Elizabeth was weeping bitterly at seeing herself so little like her crucified Love. In her desolation she turned again to these holy persons, and asked them to come to her aid. They appeared to her, and gave her the hope that she would obtain the grace which she desired. Our Lord directed towards her a ray of light, which shone upon her, and filled her with strength and courage; the Blessed John Baptist of the Immaculate Conception exhorted her by powerful words, and by the aid of these marvellous succours she took her flight, and flew into the bosom of God. Our Lord united her to Himself, and communicated to her a more perfect resemblance to His Divine Person. He promised also to bestow upon her in heaven the recompense destined for those who are enclosed in the Cloister, as a reward for the retired life which she had voluntarily led in the world.

Besides the Saints of whom we have spoken, she had also the habit of honouring by particular practices S. Joachim and S. Anne, the Blessed parents of the Mother of God; S. Zachary and S. Elizabeth, the parents of the Divine Precursor, S. Francis of Assisi, the passionate lover of the Cross; S. Francis Xavier, S. Aloysius

Gonzague, and S. Stanislaus Kotska, all three belonging to the immortal crown of her beloved Father, S. Ignatius Loyola. In fine, she honoured all the Saints who had passed from a life of sin by the laborious practices of penance; she loved to humble herself in their presence, and to protest that she was the most unworthy of sinners.

CHAPTER XV

Efficacy of the prayers of the Venerable Mother in obtaining all kinds of graces.—She converts various sinners on the way to damnation.—Miraculous cure of His Holiness Pius VII.—The gift of tears granted to Elizabeth; holy use which she makes of them.—She penetrates the secret of consciences.—Narrative of a young man on the subject of a sin recently committed.—She foretells the future of many persons.—She goes, by the gift of bilocation, to the aid of many different people.

THE intimate and frequent communications of Our Lord with Elizabeth had supernaturalised all her faculties, and raised her to that state of perfect union by which she participated in an ineffable manner in the attributes of the Divinity. The mysterious bonds of the sacred marriage contracted with Jesus Christ, the Mediator between God and Men, had communicated to her prayers an efficacy which nothing could resist. The celestial Spouse one day said to her: "Beloved daughter, what then could My love refuse you?" The magnificence of this promise was equalled by its effects.

One day Our Lord showed her a soul whom the devil already held in his mouth as a certain prey. At this sight Elizabeth uttered a cry of pity, and began to pray with incomparable ardour. Our Lord said to her: "The grace which you ask is great, but if you desire it you shall obtain it from My love."

The soul thus exposed to eternal perdition was that of a Religious who had violated the vows of his profession, and profaned the sacred character of the Diaconate, with which he had been invested. Overcome by his passions, which he had neglected to repress, he had thrown off his holy habit, and plunged into all sorts of crimes. He had at length fallen into the hands of justice, and was condemned to a convict's death. Instead of recognising the hand of a just God in the chastisement to which he had to submit, and offering the sacrifice of his life as an expiation for his sins, he blasphemed, and prepared himself to die in final impenitence.

Happily for him, the Beloved of Our Lord interposed her mediation with the Divine Mercy. Elizabeth did not cease to implore Jesus of Nazareth during the whole night which preceded the day of execution; she wept, she offered herself as a victim of expiation, she undertook to do penance for this man who thus trifled with eternity. So much zeal and charity gained their end; the hardened impenitent sinner was converted, and went resigned to execution, invoking the Holy Names of Jesus and Mary.

The prayers of the servant of God accompanied this wretched man beyond this life. The just Judge had deprived him in Purgatory of the benefit of the prayers which the faithful offered for him. But he obtained the grace to show himself to Elizabeth, and to implore her again for her prayers; she saw him surrounded by dark flames, and, touched by his horrible torments, she obtained for him the favour of participating in the suffrages of the faithful, on the Feast of Jesus of Nazareth, which took place three weeks after his execution.

The following fact is yet more worthy of admiration. A man, who had done some kindness to the Venerable Mother, was in the last struggle of his agony; his condition caused great doubts to be entertained of his salvation. The knowledge of this state of things induced Elizabeth, out of gratitude, to pray for this soul; suddenly the secret judgments of God were revealed to her; she saw that this soul would be condemned. She saw it trembling before the Sovereign Judge, who turned upon it an angry countenance. His Angel-Guardian held in his hand a small book, which contained so few good works that he scarcely dared to open it. The devil, on the other hand, carried a large volume in which he was prepared to show whole pages of wickedness.

At this spectacle the servant of God almost died of grief; she threw herself at the feet of Jesus and Mary, and represented to them, amidst a torrent of tears, that this unfortunate man had been her benefactor. What may not be done by a soul burning with love? Our Lord was appeased, and said to her: "My daughter, your prayer does violence to My Heart. Do you wish that he should be saved? Very Well, be it so." In saying these sweet words He placed a divine seal in the wound of His side, and marked the volume of

Chapter XV

Satan by a triple imprint of His precious Blood. He then ordered an Angel to throw these faults into the infinite ocean of His mercies; at the same time, He raised His Hand, and gave His blessing to the dying man.

During this solemn absolution, the son of the dying man, who was at the bedside of his father, surrounding him with every care, raised his eyes to the Picture of Jesus of Nazareth, hanging near the bed. He saw with astonishment the Ecce Homo disengage the right Hand from the cord which bound it, and bless his father! As a witness that there was no illusion in this miracle, the Hand of the Saviour remained free from its bonds.

Notwithstanding Elizabeth's retired life, these prodigies became bruited abroad, and they caused her to be visited by many persons who desired to take advantage of her interest with God, and to profit by the light with which she was favoured.

A pious Priest came one day to see her, and exposed to her the state of his conscience, asking her advice. He was so happy at the end of this interview, that he fell upon his knees before the servant of God, and prayed her to bless him.

Elizabeth was quite confused, and positively refused to give her blessing to a Priest. But by Divine Grace she understood that she was to obey, and she blessed him with the Trinitarian Scapular, whilst reciting the Magnificat. The humble Priest arose, penetrated with such a deep feeling of contrition, that he wept with joy and gratitude. Elizabeth attributed this grace to S. Michael, who had appeared to her a short time previously, and imparted to her some of his glory.

The favours which she obtained by her prayers were incalculable; it seemed that she disposed at her pleasure of heavenly treasures. The hardest hearts were touched and induced to return to virtue, barren women became fruitful, living children were given to mothers who had before only had still-born infants, maladies of all kinds and degrees were cured, resignation obtained for afflicted souls; in a word, her path was sown with blessings, and she never sojourned in a place without leaving behind her the imperishable effects of her power and her charity. So that, when the process of Beatification was opened, it was necessary to obtain information from several Dioceses at the same time, and each of them recorded fresh miracles.

It was just that the Vicar of Jesus Christ should also participate in this source of salvation, opened, as it were, at the foot of the Pontifical Throne. One day the holy and venerable Pontiff, Pius VII., had a fall, from which fatal consequences were feared. The Venerable Mother, profoundly afflicted at the news of this accident, began to pray most ardently for his cure. Our Lord ordered her to send to him a small vial of the water of Jesus of Nazareth. She desired to obey, but who would undertake to present this beneficial water to the Sovereign Pontiff? At the same moment that she conjured God to come to her aid, she found herself suddenly transported in spirit into the apartment of the Holy Father. There she saw the Three Kings, who themselves presented the miraculous water to the august patient. A few days later it was reported throughout Rome that the Holy Father had been completely cured.

In order to give more efficacy to Elizabeth's prayers, Our Lord enriched her with the gift of tears. In her long meditations they flowed abundantly.

Contemplation of the adorable mysteries of the love of God, meditation on the sufferings of Jesus during His cruel Passion, the remembrance of her own faults, which her humility exaggerated, all joined in moving her, and converting her eyes into a source of unceasing tears. When she contemplated the evils of the Church, and prayed for her deliverance from them, or when she asked for the conversion of some great sinner, whom she wished to rescue, as it were, by violence from the mouth of hell, her tears were poured forth in torrents.

The gift of penetrating into consciences, and of discovering what was there secretly passing, often furnished her with an occasion of weeping over the evils which were concealed from the rest of the world. Mary Josephine, her youngest daughter, said that

Chapter XV

neither she nor her sister, Mary Anne, could ever conceal anything from their holy mother. At the very moment that they had any secret, she revealed it to them, and threw them into a state of strange confusion.

One day one of her friends went to confession, and believed that she had told all to her spiritual Father; but Elizabeth reminded her of several faults of which she had not even thought. Several times, on meeting persons whom she had never known, she perceived that they were in a state of sin, or on the point of falling into it, and she gave them charitable advice, exhorting them to free themselves from their sin, or to preserve themselves from it.

A young man one day brought her a letter from another person. Elizabeth turned to him angrily, and said: "What! you have the audacity to salute me? Make an act of contrition, and go instantly to confession. You have the boldness to come near Jesus of Nazareth, after what you have done to offend Him on the way!" The young man, struck by these words as by a thunderbolt, trembled from head to foot, and could not help confessing to the Venerable Mother all that had happened to him, acknowledging that he had really committed this sin during the journey.

Mother Mary Josephine relates that her mother could divine, without any one speaking to her, those who were troubled by scruples, anguish, or distress of mind, and that she sought to relieve every one by her wise counsels and holy confidence; so that many pious persons, monks, nuns, and even priests, voluntarily placed themselves under her direction, and did not disdain to be enlightened by her wisdom. She also knew those who wished to do her any evil, or nourished against her any sinister design; her charity to them was tender and ingenious; and she gave herself no rest until she had rendered them good for evil.

Elizabeth's counsels were extremely valuable, because of her gift of prophecy and her knowledge of the future. How often has she foretold the cure of the sick whom the physicians believed to be in a hopeless condition, and the deaths of many whom they considered to be far from danger! One day she advised a merchant not to intrust his affairs to another, because he was sure to become bankrupt, and this he did very shortly after. A mother complained to her of the trouble which she had with one of her daughters, whose obstinate character gave her great annoyance. "You may console yourself," said the Venerable Mother, "your daughter will change, and will become a Dominican Nun." The prediction seemed very improbable, but it was fulfilled. Another was lamenting because her son showed from his infancy a hard and intractable disposition. "This child," said Elizabeth, "will one day become a holy priest, and will be the consolation and support of your family." She had foreseen the future exactly as it came to pass. A young Novice spoke to her of the fear that he had that he should not persevere in the Religious state, and of the hesitation he felt as to making his vows. Elizabeth reassured him, and foretold to him that he would remain a good Religious up to the time of his death; and in this case also her words were verified.

The following circumstance contains quite a complication of wonders. A pious mother learnt that her son had died without the succours of religion, and feared the eternal loss of this dear soul. In her distress she hastened to the Venerable Mother, who began to pray to know what had become of the soul whose condition occasioned them so much sorrow. Suddenly she saw before her the soul of Anna Maria Taigi, a person of great piety, who showed her the soul of the dead person enveloped in flames. The deceased revealed to her that he had been saved by the prayers of this other servant of God, and he wept with gratitude.

Our Lord even sent her to distant places to console the afflicted by the gift of bilocation. The Rev. Father Ferdiand of S. Louis, her Confessor, having learnt that his brother, a Carthusian in Spain, had fallen seriously ill, recommended him to the prayers of his virtuous penitent. She knew that this Religious was dying, and harassed by cruel distress of mind. She prayed for him, and Our Lord said to her: "Go, my daughter, go as a messenger of peace; announce from Me to My servant that he will soon be in Paradise with Me. As a proof of the truth of your word, I will give

Chapter XV

him peace of mind and submission to the Divine Will." In a moment she was transported in spirit into the cell of the dying Religious, announced to him the good tidings, and filled him with celestial joy. She also saw him, after his decease, glorious in heaven. At the same time she saw in the regions of celestial happiness another brother of her spiritual Father, resplendent with beauty, with a glorious palm in his hand. This Religious had been shot in defence of the Church.

But we will return to the prophetic incidents recorded in the life of Elizabeth. She made a prediction to one of her daughters, Mary Anne, that she would be established in the world, but that she would live only a short time; she was indeed married, and died two years later. To the other, Mary Josephine, she foretold that she would become a Religious, and that people would go to her convent to visit Jesus of Nazareth. She embraced the Religious life, after the death of her Venerable Mother, with the Dames Oblates of S. Philip Neri; she is now Superioress in that monastery, and shows with pleasure the miraculous picture to the faithful who desire to venerate it.

The mother of Mary Frances Paglia wished to give her daughter in marriage to a widower; Elizabeth dissuaded her, and in the course of two or three months this man died. She then engaged this girl as a lay sister for one of the Choir of the Monastery of the Infant Jesus. The girl would not follow this advice, saying that she preferred to live in the world and preserve her liberty. Elizabeth said to her: "It is true that the young lady whom you would go to serve in the Convent of the Infant Jesus will not live long; but if you remain in the world you will have to pass through many trials." The young Religious, indeed, lived only three or four years after she entered the Monastery; but the obstinate girl suffered cruel trials afterwards.

A woman of the small town of Marino, named Catherine Amadei, had recourse to Elizabeth to recommend to her prayers her husband, who was dangerously ill; the Venerable Mother consoled her by revealing to her that this illness was sent to her husband in order to ensure his salvation. "Take courage," she said to her, "and if it please God to call your husband at a favourable time, so as to rescue him from the perils of eternal damnation, to which he would be exposed if his life were to be prolonged, would you trouble yourself for this, and would you oppose the Divine Will? If Our Lord take your husband, He will Himself provide for you what is necessary, and for your two sons whom he will leave." The woman became resigned, and, in the course of two or three days, her husband died.

Elizabeth became the confidential adviser in all sorts of troubles. Angela Ferroni, of Marino, came in tears to relate to her that her betrothed had deserted her, and that, not content with this odious infidelity, he had added to it injuries and insults. Moved with compassion, Elizabeth led her into the presence of Jesus of Nazareth, and made her renounce all resentment and desire of revenge. Then she said to her: "Although this young man has already published his intended marriage with another person, he will return to you and marry you. But I fear that severe trials await you." The marriage took place contrary to all probability, but the second portion of the prediction was accomplished as well as the first.

A man named De Sanctis, of Marino, lost a splendid mare, which he valued exceedingly. The sorrow he experienced, added to the extraordinary exertion which he had made to find it, caused him to fall dangerously ill. His son, Matthew de Sanctis, distressed by his father's condition, went to Rome to see the Venerable Mother, and in her presence gave way to uncontrollable grief.

Elizabeth, much moved, led the young man to her Oratory, and told him to recite three Paters and three Aves in honour of the Three Kings, with the assurance that he would recover the lost mare. After some other prayers to Jesus of Nazareth she informed him that his father was already better. Then she said to him: "Listen, Matthew, where do you wish the mare to be left if she should be recovered? Would you like her to be taken to your friend, John Fioravanti?" The young man replied that he would

Chapter XV

like this to be done.

Seven or eight days after the son of De Sanctis returned to Rome, and, to his great satisfaction, he found the animal in the stable of his friend Fioravanti. He asked the coachman who brought her. He told him that the animal was brought back by a well-dressed young peasant, and that when he went to seek him to give him a reward he was not to be found. Matthew de Sanctis hastened to Elizabeth to inform her of what had occurred, and to thank her. She replied to him: "Go, and return thanks to Jesus of Nazareth and the Three Kings."

The realisation of the following prophecy was a cause of great admiration to those who witnessed it. Elizabeth had told her daughter Mary that one day one of her nephews would make himself very active on her behalf. On entering the convent Mary communicated this prediction to her companions. All the Religious waited impatiently for this nephew who should glorify the Venerable Mother, but more than forty years had passed since this announcement had been made, and he had not yet appeared! One day a revolutionary storm drove into Rome a Brother of the Christian Schools, Louis Canori—in Religion, Brother Romuald—who then heard for the first time that he was the nephew of a most holy woman. He immediately undertook to institute the Ordinary Process for her canonisation, and displayed so much activity and zeal that he had the happiness to see his labours crowned with success. The Process, beginning on the 6th September, 1864, ended in the month of July, 1867. As to himself, he only heard of the prophecy of which he was the subject during that time.

The gift of bilocation with which Elizabeth was endowed enabled her more than once to render valuable services. Rosa Terribile, of the town of Marino, was one day in the house of Jacqueline, her relative, and was conversing with her in her room. Suddenly Jacqueline's daughter uttered a piercing cry in the next room. Her mother, instead of going to help her, contented herself by saying: "If anything has happened to her, so much the better!

Why is she so impertinent?" At that moment they distinctly heard Elizabeth's voice calling, "Jacqueline! Jacqueline!" Rose and Jacqueline ran as fast as they could, but Elizabeth was not there, and they found the young girl with her hand fastened down by the lid of a box in such a way that she could not withdraw it. They quickly raised the lid, and the hand, which seemed to be broken, was not even discoloured. The two women attributed this visible protection to Elizabeth's prayers; but she referred them, as usual, to Jesus of Nazareth.

CHAPTER XVI

The Venerable Mother is privileged to deliver a great many souls from Purgatory.—Our Lord gives His servant the keys of Purgatory.—She delivers from Purgatory the members of her family, and particularly Cardinal Scotti.—She goes into Purgatory on the Feast of All Saints, and frees a great many suffering souls.—Glorious triumph which she obtains in their favour in the year of her death.

AMONG the greatest of the wonderful privileges with which the Venerable Mother was endowed, was that of holding at her disposal, in a manner, the keys of Purgatory, and of delivering from thence a great number of souls.

On the day when the Triduum was celebrated in Rome, in honour of the Beatification of the servant of God, John Baptist of the Immaculate Conception, the Reformer of the Order of barefooted Trinitarians, Elizabeth prayed for a soul that was very dear to her. Our Lord appeared to her and said: "Take the keys, which in My mercy I have already several times placed at your disposal, open the horrible prison of Purgatory, and, through the merits of My Blessed servant, John Baptist, I shall be pleased to deliver a great many souls."

These words were scarcely ended when she saw coming to her the Blessed John Baptist, with S. Felix of Valois and S. John of Matha, accompanied by two Angels who had the guard of Purgatory. The humble Elizabeth respectfully gave the keys to these Angels, who immediately entered with the Saints into the sombre dungeons of Divine Justice. The Blessed John Baptist of the Immaculate Conception set at liberty more than three hundred souls, and among them the one for whom Elizabeth had prayed.

This phalanx came to Elizabeth, escorted by a considerable number of Angels, who, rejoicing, sang a hymn of triumph, and all together took their flight to heaven, under the form of three luminous and burning globes. At this sight Elizabeth wished to follow them, but her hour was not yet come. When she found herself detained in this land of exile by the weight of human misery, she wept so bitterly that the Blessed Virgin was touched with pity, and came to console her.

"My daughter," she said, "consent to remain yet awhile here, so as to accomplish the most holy Will of God. He wishes you to become a faithful imitator of my beloved son, John Baptist of the Immaculate Conception, and by your means to save a great number of souls. I will protect you and serve as your Advocate in all your wants. Invoke my Name, and I will help you." She then added: "Look at me." Elizabeth, always modest, had cast down her eyes out of respect to the Queen of Heaven. She looked, and she saw the Blessed Virgin dressed in the habit of the Order of the Most Holy Trinity. She then said to her: "I am the protectress and foundress of the Order of the Blessed Trinity." At these words she disappeared, leaving Elizabeth filled with heavenly peace and joy.

Elizabeth charitably interested herself for all departed souls, but especially for those of her own relatives.

On the 24th January, 1807, the holy Patriarch of the Seraphic Order informed her that on the next day her father would sleep in Our Lord. He gave her this information in order to recompense Signor Canori for the services which he had given to the Religious of Ara Cœli whilst acting as their Syndic—that is to say, their temporal administrator. Elizabeth forgot nothing that would dispose the venerable old man for a holy death. She did not cease praying for his soul, until she knew that he was in Glory. Her father one day appeared to her after Holy Communion, resplendent with light; he congratulated her on the graces which Our Lord had so bountifully bestowed upon her, and recommended her to pray for her other deceased relatives.

Faithful to this advice, she procured a Mass for their souls, and had the happiness of seeing fifteen take their flight to heaven, accompanied by their Angels-Guardian. We have seen how hard and severe her step-father, Dr. Mora, had been towards her during the last years of his life. But her angelic heart did not preserve the least resentment, and, when he left this world, she abridged for him considerably the cruel tortures of Purgatory. It is our duty to say that Dr. Mora was a good man, imbued with the fear of God, and full of charity for the poor. He even took measures to relieve them, after his death, by pious legacies.

Elizabeth's pious mother remained until 1821; at this time, Our Lord required from her this sacrifice. Signora Canori was a benefactress of the Seraphic Order; and S. Francis came to inform her daughter that she would appear the next day before God, so that she might prepare her for the terrible passage. She had scarcely closed her eyes than Elizabeth began to pray for her with the greatest fervour. Our Lord, touched by the depth of her filial piety, told her that this dear soul would be delivered on the day that she would cause a Mass to be celebrated in the Oratory of Jesus of Nazareth. Elizabeth had this precious Mass celebrated without delay, and when she was receiving Holy Communion she had the inexpressible joy of seeing the soul of her beloved mother, resplendent with glory, take its flight to heaven, accompanied by its Angel-Guardian.

On the 12th December, 1824, she lost her mother-in-law, who had always loved her so tenderly, and had never taken any part in the unkind treatment of the rest of the family towards her. Gratitude imposed on Elizabeth the duty of causing the Holy Sacrifice to be several times celebrated for her. This being not yet sufficient to rescue her from the cruel flames of Purgatory, she offered herself to God as a victim, so as to suffer herself all the torments necessary for her deliverance.

Our Lord, touched by this heroic act of generosity, said to her: "The soul for which you pray will be delivered on the day when a Priest shall come of himself to celebrate Mass in your chapel." Elizabeth immediately applied herself to obtain from God the visit of this desired Priest. In the course of a few days a Camaldolese Priest presented himself, and said: "Our Lord has inspired me to come here to celebrate Mass." Elizabeth understood, and trembled with joy.

At the moment when she received Holy Communion she saw the soul of her mother-in-law glorified rising to heaven.

She interested all the Saints whom she honoured with a special devotion in favour of these dear souls in Purgatory.

One day, when the Feast of S. Michael the Archangel was being celebrated, she offered, through his hands, to the Eternal Father, the precious Blood of Our Lord, and obtained the deliverance of thirty-three souls, who had been zealous, during their lifetime, for the glory of this Archangel and that of the Queen of Heaven.

When one of her friends, named Anna Maria Taigi, quitted this life of pain and trial, Elizabeth saw her take her flight to heaven, between S. John of Matha and S. Felix of Valois. The Blessed Virgin came to meet her, and Our Lord invested her with splendour and glory.

Before disappearing and becoming for ever lost in the ocean of Divine Perfection, this blessed soul turned to Elizabeth ravished in ecstasy, and warned her to prepare herself to receive from Our Lord a signal favour.

Elizabeth was extremely devoted to all the Clergy, but particularly to the Sacred College of Cardinals, who are as the supports of the Church, the eyes and arms of the Apostolic See. She ardently prayed for them during their life and after their death. One day when she went to Holy Communion for the pious Cardinal Scotti, the soul of this eminent personage appeared to her, and said: "I thank you for having abridged my sufferings by means of yours; I am going to Paradise."

One day, on a Feast of all Saints, she was praying with her usual fervour for the souls of the departed, in the Church of S. Charles, when suddenly a large key was presented to her, and she heard the words: "Go, and deliver at your own choice as many as you please." At the same time S. Charles and the holy Founders of the Trinitarian Order appeared to her, and offered to conduct her to Purgatory. The sight of the horrible pains which the holy souls endured deeply moved the compassionate heart of Elizabeth. Our Lord showing Himself in this frightful abode, she threw herself at His feet, and asked of Him so ardently the deliverance of these suffering souls, that our Divine Saviour set at liberty an extraordinary number.

The Octave of All Saints being consecrated by the Church to the relief of the departed, the Venerable Mother neglected no means of aiding them. She obtained the deliverance of an incalculable number of souls on the days when the anniversary services were celebrated for them. Many of them had been aggregated to the Third Order of the Blessed Trinity; others belonged to all states and conditions. She saw these souls rising to heaven, following their Guardian-Angels in groups so numerous that it seemed that Purgatory must have become empty.

Nothing could equal the triumph which she achieved the last time that she celebrated this pious Octave: that is to say, in 1824. Whilst she was praying the Divine Lamb to display His mercy in regard of these holy souls, Our Lord replied: "I grant you the grace which you ask, according to the measure of your desires. Deliver from Purgatory as many souls as you wish." Elizabeth, delighted, could not contain herself for joy. But, diffident of herself, and desiring to use the power which was given her according to the Divine Will, she prayed the adorable Saviour to accompany her, and He granted her this favour. Arrived in these burning cells, she conceived such excessive grief at the sight of such horrible tortures that she begged for mercy for all these unfortunate souls.

Our Lord said to her: "Beloved daughter, place your hand in the wound of My Heart, and bring out an abundance of Blood." Elizabeth obeyed, and the torrents of the adorable Blood, escaping from this Sacred Source, inundated the whole of Purgatory, and the number of souls who were delivered was so great that the Venerable Mother might believe that no more remained in suffering.

The Feast of Our Lady of the Portiuncula was also a day blessed for the suffering souls; she delivered them in troops. There were also other days in the year when the God of Mercy condescended to listen to her earnest prayers, and granted to her the deliverance of captives. The holy souls in Purgatory are the Elect of Our Lord, the Spouses of the Great King, the future heirs of heavenly glory; Our Lord only desires that they may quickly enter into His kingdom. He is ready to listen to all who will interest themselves for them, and He bestows precious graces upon the faithful who abridge their painful exile.

CHAPTER XVII

Our Lord shows, by symbolical visions, to the Venerable Mother the care which He lavishes upon her soul.—Her ardent desire for perfection, and the graces which she obtains.—She makes the Religious vows, and rigorously observes them.—Rule of Life.—She practises it with great perfection.—Elizabeth makes a vow to do what seems to be most perfect. Severity of her penance.—Our Lord draws up for her a more austere Rule of Life.

OUR Lord condescended to show to Elizabeth the tender cares which He lavished upon her soul, and He appeared to her under the form of an active and vigilant gardener. He first eradicated from His garden all the weeds, and then went to wash His Hands in a fountain, whose waters, mingled with the precious Blood which flowed from His adorable Wounds, soon became of a purple colour. He used this water to water all the plants, and it penetrated to the roots, and gave vigour to the leaves and fruit. Whilst this picture passed before her eyes, Elizabeth experienced a secret operation which purified her soul.

Another time the Divine Saviour offered Himself to her under the gracious image of the Tree of Life: she saw the three powers of His Soul, Understanding, Memory, and Will, closely united in this tree, and forming three branches covered with all sorts of fruits. Our Lord then said to His faithful servant: "Look at these precious fruits hanging from these branches. These are the fruits of My Divine Grace." This great goodness on the part of her God had enkindled in Elizabeth an inexpressible desire to correspond more entirely with Divine Grace; she would willingly support every torment rather than be faithless. "O my God," she exclaimed, "O my Love, I offer you my blood and my life; give me correspondence and perfection." Another familiar exclamation was this: "O Lord, perfection or death."

To second the efforts of her will. Our Lord bestowed upon her the three degrees of humility, which freed her from the perverse inclinations of corrupt nature. After this supernatural operation, her conscience became of an angelic purity and delicacy. She always feared that sin might glide into her heart unknown to herself, and watched carefully over all the movements of her soul. Above all, she always kept her eyes open as regarded her affections, knowing the holy jealousy of Our Lord. God alone, and the entire accomplishment of His Divine Will, became her only object. Moved by the generosity with which Elizabeth devoted herself to His glory, Our Lord imparted to her the gift of knowledge, so that she understood the true nature of Christian perfection, and the most efficacious means of attaining to it. The Divine light which penetrated her opened to her a new horizon, and showed her virtue under a more attractive aspect. Thus her desire for sanctity was so much inflamed that God pleased to come to her aid by another prodigy.

One day, on a Feast of S. John the Baptist, being unable to support the thought of her supposed infidelity, she threw herself at the feet of this glorious Saint, protesting that she desired at any price to repair the treasons and infidelities which she had been guilty of towards Infinite Love. She offered herself to suffer every kind of torment so that they might be forgotten. Our Lord instantly granted her three new degrees of perfection, which He infused into her soul.

But this astonishing liberality, far from appeasing the insatiable ardour of the Venerable Mother, served only to increase it. In 1804, she conceived the idea of making the three vows of Evangelical Perfection, so as to obtain, whilst living in the world, the advantages attached to the sanctity of the Cloister. Such a determination was heroic; but her manner of putting it into practice is still more worthy of admiration.

Regarding chastity, she possessed it in a degree evidently miraculous. One day the Rev. Father Ferdinand questioned her on this point, and she replied: "My Father, for the last sixteen years, by the grace of God, I have not had even a single thought contrary to this virtue. I am to-day twenty-nine years of age, and I declare to you that I never suffer the slightest annoyance in this respect. My heart has no desire or attraction but to the love of Our Lord Jesus Christ. The devils have tormented me in every way, but never on this point, for which I am ready to give my blood and my life. They have not obtained that power from God." Such a degree of virtue can only proceed from a special privilege with which God pleases to honour some souls. It does not depend upon any one to acquire such a grace; and God, Who is all-powerful, can also sanctify a soul amid the most painful and laborious struggles, as well as in the midst of unalterable peace. Here the servant of God is more to be admired than imitated; but every one can follow her footsteps as regards the precautions with which she surrounded herself so as to ensure the guardianship of her precious treasure.

The two great enemies of the angelic virtue are the affections of the heart, and the wandering of the eyes. Elizabeth had prudently rendered her heart inaccessible to creatures, by accustoming it to enjoy only Divine Love. She had received from nature an extremely tender soul; but she had given a direction to its impulses, and had fixed it upon God. She was extremely careful not to allow her affections to wander or to lavish themselves upon created objects; this was for her a matter of long and severe examination. Her exterior deportment was regulated by the virtue of modesty; the angelic Elizabeth never looked any one in the face, and she scarcely knew by sight either her relatives or her intimate friends.

Towards the end of her life, when she was hardly able to leave her own house, her Confesssr had to go to visit her at home, and had frequent conversations with her regarding the marvellous operations of her soul; nevertheless, she distinguished him only by the tone of his voice.

The virtue of modesty had spread over her an inexpressible charm. Her eyes were always cast down, but without constraint or effort; in fact, this seemed to be their natural condition. Her mind seemed to be always recollected, and sweetly resting upon God. She never made a hasty movement; her actions were all gentle and quiet; her countenance was open and candid, expressing the sentiments of her soul. She spoke little; but her words were agreeable, and she said a great deal in a few words.

All these virtues rendered her an object of veneration to those who approached her. The boldest men felt themselves constrained to be respectful in her presence, and not one of them would have had the temerity to say before her one word in the slightest degree indecorous. When Our Lord announced to her some terrible illness to appease His just anger, one of the most earnest requests which she made to her daughters was that they would themselves take care of her, and not allow any one else to touch her. She even requested them to clothe her with their own hands after her death, thus showing herself chaste and modest even in her tomb. She had brought up her daughters with the same feelings and habits.

The rigour with which she practised the vow of poverty was not less admirable. She had only very few clothes, and all of poor and common material. Her ordinary costume was a dress of black stuff, and a cotton tunic. She had kept a few coarse linen chemises, but she did not wear them, even when she was sick. Her relations obliged her to have a silk dress, but she only wore it when they ordered her to do so. She did not undertake the disposal of anything: she gave up to her daughters the care of the house, and when she required anything, she asked for it from them.

Her bed served merely as an ornament to her room, and to conceal her penances. She slept on the floor, upon a mattress made of hair, with a single cotton covering. She modified this austere habit only in times of sickness, when she allowed those who had the care of her to place her on her bed.

She carried the practice of poverty so far as to use carefully the most common and valueless things. One day, when her daughters saw her economising even the water, they expressed their surprise to her. "Ah! my children," she said, "I desire to use as little as possible of created things." She would not even bestow an alms without the consent of her daughters. Through the fear of distressing them by showing too great dependence on them, she said: "I ask you this, my children, because my head is not always clear, and I forget what should be given to a poor person in such or such a situation."

She practised obedience without limit or restriction, embracing this virtue in all its perfection, from the moment that she determined to give herself altogether to God. One of the first sacrifices which she made in consecrating herself to His service was that of her will and her judgment. This heroic offering corresponded with the time when she left her sumptuous habitation in the Vespignani Palace, in obedience to her father-in-law, to live in a modest room which he had himself rented for her. She then entered her mother-in-law's family, and hastened to take up the position of a simple daughter obedient in all things. She did not stop here; the household was composed of more than thirteen persons, and she resolved to regard them all as her superiors, even the servants. She promised this to God, and she faithfully kept her word.

Human nature is so constituted that, from the moment when any person, in a community or a family, consecrates himself to the practice of perfect obedience, every one claims his services, and believes he has a right to command them. The virtue of obedience is so precious, that even those who do not practise it esteem and love it in others, and desire to exercise it for their own profit. Thus it was in the respectable Mora family. Every one required Elizabeth's time, every one pretended that the others did not keep her sufficiently occupied, and used her as if each one had a right to her services. The servants, seeing that she came promptly to aid them in their troubles, often had recourse to her assistance, even for the lowest and most abject offices in the house.

Elizabeth obeyed so promptly and cheerfully, that none thought they could become troublesome to her. Modest and calm, she went everywhere where she was called; undertaking or leaving any work with unalterable serenity. When it was seen that she was always ready to do the will of others, it was said that she had no will of her own, and that, by a particular privilege, she had the gift of allowing herself to be ordered by whoever chose to do so.

The perfection of her incomparable obedience consisted in this, that she willingly attributed every failure to her own fault, and generously left to others the glory of all that was well done. All that was wrong was imputed to her, and all that she did well was turned to the praise of others; and, as a natural consequence, she received few compliments, but frequent reproaches. All was alike to her noble heart; the most unjust reprimands seemed to her even preferable, because they rendered her more like Our Lord, so often outraged in return for the proofs which He continually gives us of His infinite love. When she had again become mistress of her own house, she would not break the sweet and soft yoke of obedience, and, in order to preserve this precious treasure, she discovered the secret of submitting herself to her daughters, as it were, without their own knowledge.

Her dependence upon her Confessor is also worthy of admiration. Father Ferdinand put her virtue to a dreadful trial when she asked his permission to renew her vow of chastity. Twice he ordered her to offer her husband to renounce her vow. She would have suffered less in going to martyrdom; nevertheless, she obeyed her Confessor. Divine Providence watched over her, and her husband left her in a state of entire liberty. Our Lord had already foreshown her this unhoped-for result, and had said to her: "Fear nothing, My daughter; I will protect you. You are consecrated to Me; I will take care of you." Her Confessor then hesitated no longer, and authorised her to renew the vow which she had made in her childhood.

One evening, being ravished in God, the abundance of consolation which she enjoyed was extreme. She would willingly have passed the night in this state of ineffable happiness; but knowing that this was forbidden by her Confessor, she went promptly to bed. Her Confessor had also forbidden her to offer herself to the Divine Justice, so as to appease His anger by new sufferings, without having previously obtained his approbation. One day, during an ecstasy, when she saw the Saviour ready to discharge the most terrible punishments upon the human race, she forgot the order which she had received, and offered herself as a victim of expiation for many of these ungrateful and abominable sinners. When she remembered afterwards that she had violated a formal command of holy obedience, she fell into such an excess of grief that she became inconsolable. She hastened to prostrate herself at the feet of her worthy Father, and there shed such a torrent of tears, that he, deeply moved, knew not how to stay their course.

In order to attain to this sublime perfection, Elizabeth had composed a little summary of resolutions, which she made the basis of her conduct. These resolves are so much to her praise, that we will here transcribe them. These are her own words:

"I will keep myself unceasingly in the presence of God. I will not allow myself to be irritated by any injury or affront, however painful it may be to human nature; I will receive all with submission and joy from the hand of Our Lord."

"I will never desire any good or advantage, but that which is spiritual; and conform myself solely to the Divine Will."

"I will exercise myself in the practices of mortification, of penance, of humility, meekness, patience, longanimity, love of suffering, and deprivation of all which may please or flatter the senses."

"I will take care not to place my confidence in any human aid; I will rely only on the merits of Our Lord Jesus Christ, and the pure bounty of Our Lord."

"I desire that every breath that I draw may be an act of love of God, and of sorrow for having offended Him; and as so many acts of offering of myself to all kinds of sacrifice and suffering, and even death itself, to bear witness to my love, and obtain the conversion of all those who have the misfortune not to know Him."

"I will exercise myself in all theological and moral virtues; I will foster a great desire to be humiliated and oppressed. I will endeavour to rejoice amid insults and unjust reproaches. I will make a determination to die entirely to myself, so as to live only the life of Jesus Crucified; henceforth I will seek only the Cross, the thorns and the nails."

She placed the seal upon these admirable promises by a vow of practising always, in all things, that which was most perfect.

Elizabeth had all these points constantly before her eyes; they were approved by her Director, and she never deviated from them in any way. A soul imbued with the fear of God is not more attentive to observe the commandments of God and of the Church than Elizabeth was to observe the laws which her love had imposed on her. She examined herself without ceasing regarding her fidelity to their practice; and if she thought she had been negligent—not in a literal sense, for this never occurred, but in what was most sublime and perfect in these laws—she conceived a sorrow and regret, which she manifested outwardly by torrents of tears. More than once she gave way to her grief, and fell down in a fainting fit; for Divine light had so enlightened her mind as to the greatness of the offences committed against the Majesty of God, that the mere shadow of sin would have caused her death.

Even the words of her spiritual Father did not always suffice to console her in her distress, and Our Lord had to come to her aid. He appeared to her, and told her with the tender accent of Infinite Goodness: "My beloved daughter, your faults do not harm either you or Me. My graces are neither diminished nor retarded: I grant them all to you, without discussing your merits, and in virtue of My infinite love for you."

Elizabeth, ever persuaded that she was the greatest sinner in the world, could never satisfy herself with macerations and penances; they were the food of her life, and if a vigilant direction had not kept her within just bounds, she would never have believed that she had done enough. In her visits to the hospitals, she sought out the most repulsive of the sick, and rendered them services so painful to her delicate nature, that her stomach often rose violently against them. She laughed at what she called her weakness, and returned to the charge with a sweet face, and an angelic smile upon her lips.

She courageously supported the oppressive heat of summer and the cruel cold of winter, without ever doing anything that would bring her relief. She would endure the most intense thirst, without ever taking anything to assuage it; she remained absolutely without drinking from the evening of Friday to mid-day on Saturday, in honour of the Sacred Thirst of Jesus on the Cross. Her fasts were frequent and rigorous; she passed entire Novenas, taking only a cup of chocolate and a small piece of bread every day; sometimes she took this nourishment only on every second day. Before her Director moderated her pious excesses, she prolonged her prayer for five or six hours, never ceasing, during the whole time, to exercise cruelties upon herself.

During the last ten years of her life, Our Lord pleased to grant more abundant food to her thirst for suffering, and He Himself increased the amount of her austerities. He ordered her to leave the hair mattress, and to sleep on the bare ground. He also desired her to fast continually, contenting herself with a soup of boiled herbs and some meagre food of a coarser kind. She thus ended in the most severe penance a life wholly angelic.

CHAPTER XVIII

The three theological virtues are the necessary foundation of sanctity.—All the Saints necessarily possessed these virtues in a heroic degree.—Wonderful operations of Divine Grace in creating Faith, Hope, and Charity in the Venerable Mother.—Her ardent charity towards her neighbour.

THE three theological virtues are the necessary foundation of the Christian life, and the perfection with which they are practised by a soul indicates the true measure of sanctity. So that the Church in the Process which she institutes regarding the virtue of the servants of God, always begins by examining if they possessed in a heroic degree Faith, Hope, and Charity. And if she does not find in their lives certain proofs of their having highly possessed these Virtues, although they may have accomplished numerous and striking miracles, she will never grant them the honour of canonisation.

Our Lord, designing to make Elizabeth Canori Mora an accomplished model of sanctity for the present time, multiplied in her the operations of His grace, so as to elevate Faith, Hope, and her Charity to that sublime degree which excited the admiration and obtained the suffrages of all.

After one of these ineffable operations the servant of God wrote to her Director: "Faith gives me the knowledge of the Almighty Works of God; Hope gives me an entire confidence in the Sovereign Good; and Charity makes me love God with all the strength and all the powers of my poor heart."

Divine liberality was not confined to this first gift. With the view of recompensing her fidelity and giving value to this precious talent, He confided to her three others, that is to say, that Our Lord raised these three virtues in her to a high degree of perfection. Her Faith received celestial wings, and raised her to the heights of the most inaccessible mysteries. Her heightened intelligence, like that of the Cherubim, enabled her to penetrate the depths of the Divine purposes, and contemplate the sublime end for which Our Lord had left the immovable repose of His eternity to create all things.

The mystery of the Most Blessed Trinity was no longer impenetrable to her. God, one in Nature, and three in Person, was manifested to her mind under the symbol of a boundless and unfathomable Ocean of pure light, divided into three globes of inexpressible beauty. The sight of this Supreme Majesty entirely transformed her, filling her heart with love, gratitude, and adoration. The presence of this incomparable greatness made her comprehend the reality of her nothingness, and created in her soul an abyss of humility.

Whilst she was contemplating the three Attributes of the Divinity, Power, Wisdom, and Love, three rays, like lightning, shot forth from the three luminous globes, and wholly penetrated her. She then felt herself filled with God, and was enlightened regarding the number and greatness of the graces which had been bestowed upon her.

This sublime vision inspired Elizabeth with a profound devotion to the Blessed Trinity. She invoked it without ceasing, and zealously applied herself to induce others to make these invocations; she made use of the following aspirations:

"Most Holy Trinity, I believe in you, and I confess you, as you are in truth. Gloria Patri, etc."

"Most Holy Trinity, I hope to be saved by your goodness. Gloria Patri, etc."

"Most Holy Trinity, this heart which loves you now will love you eternally. Gloria Patri, etc."

"Most Holy Trinity, I implore your mercy for every negligence committed against the Divinity. Gloria Patri, etc."

"Most Holy Trinity, grant me this grace from pure charity. Gloria Patri, etc."

Each of the three theological virtues had produced most wonderful effects in Elizabeth. Solitude, which gave her facilities for keeping herself in the presence of God, had for her inexpressible charms; she called it her Paradise on earth. Her intention was always holy and pure; all that she did was inspired by zeal for the glory of God, and raised her to Him as naturally as the perfume of incense.

She invoked God by continual prayer, sometimes asking Him for strength necessary to fight against the infernal spirits, sometimes for the triumph of the Church over her enemies, sometimes for the graces which she had been asked to solicit. From her childhood she had delighted in meditating on the mysteries of our Holy Religion; she prayed for the Propagation of the Faith, and the cessation of the persecutions of which the Church was the object. She boldly confessed her Faith, not before the tyrants of the world, for there was no occasion to do this, but before the powers of hell, and in defiance of all the sufferings which their rage could invent.

When she spoke of holy things she seemed to be transported beyond herself, as if she actually beheld the truths which she conversed upon. She could not endure any ignorance of our adorable mysteries; if she met with any one who was not instructed, she immediately began to teach him herself. In cases where she could not do so, as when she was only passing through a place, she would confide these persons to the care of some pious soul, or to some virtuous and zealous Priest. She would not allow any one to speak in her presence against Religion, or the Sovereign Pontiff, or the Clergy. Although gentle and modest, she then took a high tone; and imposed silence with so much authority that the boldest were confounded and remained mute. She corrected, without respect of persons, all that she heard contrary to Catholic truth.

She possessed the virtue of Hope in the highest degree; she had attained to a loving confidence which nothing could trouble or alter. This sweet and precious feeling took possession of her heart upon an Easter Sunday, by an operation of Divine Grace. When bestowing upon her this inestimable gift Our Lord said to her: "This favour, my daughter, will be very useful to you, as well as to all who are kind to you."

Nothing could diminish in her this tender and filial confidence. The sight of God in anger penetrated her with an inexpressible fear, but she flew and placed herself before Him to receive herself the awards of His awful Justice.

The cruel trials through which she passed did not in the least alter the feelings of her heart; she gave herself up with as much joy to the Divine Justice as to His love, or rather, she made no distinction: all that came to her from the Hand of God was equally agreeable.

The thought of her faults caused her immense suffering, and made her shed bitter tears; but never did she experience any temptation to despair. In the depth of her distress she felt the confidence that filled her heart and dilated it with celestial happiness. The devils tried every means to deprive her of a feeling which made all their efforts powerless, but they always experienced shameful defeats.

Even the anger of God could not disturb these beautiful dispositions of her soul. Our Lord had revealed to her several times that He would not listen to her prayers, and ordered her not to offer her supplications to Him. Yet she persevered in her demands with the firm conviction that she should conquer, and more than once she carried off a glorious triumph.

No one was more diffident of herself than Elizabeth; but, when relying upon the merits of Jesus Christ, she felt herself capable of moving heaven and earth.

She said to Our Lord: "My Jesus, I distrust myself, but my hope is all founded upon Thee. Yes, I am sure of it; I shall be saved by the infinite merits of Jesus. My Heavenly Father will not regard my poverty and my demerits, but He will consider the wounds of my Lord Jesus Christ." The virtue of Hope displayed itself in her to such a degree that no one could converse with her without becoming filled with confidence in God, as much with regard to temporal as to spiritual things. She would say: "Be diffident of your own weakness, and rely upon God, and you will see that all will be well."

But Charity was the virtue which most bountifully adorned the Venerable Mother and entirely possessed her. The frequent

Chapter XVIII

wounds of love which she received from the Hand of Our Lord had transformed her into a true terrestrial Seraph. She had reposed on the Bosom and in the Heart of her Good Master, like another beloved disciple.

The only fear that she experienced was that she should not correspond to the love of God. Elizabeth had only to form a desire to see it accomplished; it seemed that heaven itself was in waiting to procure for her what she desired. One day the Blessed Virgin appeared to her, and taking a beautiful pearl from her heart, she placed it in the heart of Elizabeth, Whilst making her this present she said to her: "My daughter, this is a spark of my Charity. You have only now to co-operate with this gift, and you will greatly love the Divine Majesty." Elizabeth felt that the mysterious pearl dilated in her heart, and entirely filled her, and in this manner she became a participator in the Charity of the Mother of Beautiful Love.

Charity reigned supreme in this seraphic soul. God lived in her, and directed all her actions and all her motives.

One day, after Holy Communion, the adorable Saviour suddenly revealed Himself to her, and appeared to her seated in her heart as in the throne of His Love, and surrounded by a numerous court of angelic spirits; He added these words: "Oh! Jane Felicia of My Heart, it is My delight to communicate to you My own life; make it your happiness for Me ta live in you."

These arrows of love were so many burning darts which pierced Elizabeth's heart, and transformed her into a furnace of charity. She lived no longer but for God, and the world was a burden to her. She observed silence, so as not to interrupt her communications with her Beloved, the only joy of her soul. She opened her lips only to bless and to praise Him, and her burning words touched all hearts.

The ardour of her love displayed itself exteriorly and illuminated her whole countenance. Everything revealed to her the perfections of God, and spoke to her of His infinite love in language so ardent and penetrating that she could not bear its ardour. The sight of a flower opening its beautiful calyx to the rays of the sun; a fruit hanging from the branch which had produced it; the murmur of a fountain and its limpid waters; the warbling of the birds, sufficed to throw her into an ecstasy, or would even cause her to fall suddenly to the ground, from the force of her love and adoration.

One day, in a rigorous winter, her daughters asked her why, in such intense cold, she did not come near the fire. "Ah! my children," she simply replied, "you do not know then of the flame which everywhere accompanies me? The fire which burns within me is so intense that I never feel the cold." During her meditation she could not contain her transports; night or day, she might be heard to exclaim: "Oh! how sweet it is to love God! O Love! O Charity! If every one knew Thee! Oh! how beautiful it is to serve God! O Lord! enlighten us!"

In the last years of her life her union with God was so great that a state of ecstasy became almost habitual to her; so that she could scarcely venture to go far from home through the fear of becoming an object of surprise to others. To hear of offences committed against God penetrated her with the most lively sorrow; she would change colour as if she had heard of some great misfortune. It was touching to hear her speak of our Heavenly Father, and of the love which He has shown to us, in giving us His Son, and in accepting us as His children. She treated this sublime subject with a richness of expression and an abundance of feeling which astonished those who heard her.

The love of God engendered the love of her neighbour. The two loves were united, and one was the measure of the other. We are not astonished that Elizabeth had the love of her neighbour in a heroic degree; if it were necessary for her to help another, no matter what it might cost her, she thought of neither the trouble nor the sacrifice.

One day, when going to attend the exercises of a Novena, she met a young girl who asked an alms of her. An interior inspiration persuaded her to return home to give her some help; but the fear of losing the Novena made her pass on. However, a secret remorse reproached her for having been hard to one in trouble. Divine Providence again sent this young woman in her way, and she learnt that the poor girl had on the same day escaped a great peril, caused by her having no means of living. Elizabeth, on hearing this fact, struck her breast and wept bitterly, as if she had committed the greatest crime. She desired to repair her fault, and in order that the God of Charity should forget it she undertook the support of the poor girl, without considering that she herself was poor, and required the assistance of others. Our Lord took pleasure in seeing His servant so generously squander her little pittance among His necessitous and suffering members, and in order to give her the means of continuing her bounties, He multiplied the bread, the oil, the vegetables, etc.

Signora Mora, her worthy mother-in-law, seconded, according to her power, the charitable inclinations of her daughter-in-law, and sent her money to help the poor; but Elizabeth quickly spent these small resources. The sight of the poor so distressed her that she opened wide her little purse, and often found her money in it again after having distributed it. The coins thus miraculously substituted were new and bright, as if fresh from the mint.

She often said to her daughter, now a nun, that she could not bear the pain which the distress of others caused her, and that she would willingly give up her own clothes to cover them. She did not confine herself to words; more than once she put in practice this heroic act of spoliation. Nevertheless, notwithstanding her good will and the miraculous aid of Divine Providence, she could not relieve all the distressed. Then she would throw herself at the feet of God, and conjure Him to inspire some rich person with the charitable thought of coming to her aid. She joined spiritual to temporal charity, exhorting the unfortunate to patience and resignation, with ardent and touching words; she made them appreciate their condition, and taught them to make it profitable to their salvation. Her words sank into their hearts, and opened to them an unknown source of hope and consolation; the poor came away from her, not only relieved, but in better dispositions.

Love for her neighbour produced in Elizabeth an ardent zeal for the salvation of souls. She never ceased her prayers, sighs, and supplications to obtain the conversion of sinners, and she often procured for them singular graces, of a most elevated order. The thought that so many infidel nations knew not God filled her soul with grief. If sacred duties had not detained her, she would have flown to the most savage nations on earth to procure for them the gift of Faith. To die in the most cruel torments in order to extend the Empire of the Church appeared to her the most desirable end. Being unable to attain to such a glorious martyrdom, she offered herself as a victim to Our Lord, so that, by merit and suffering, she might do what she could not realise by apostolic action.

God, Who in His goodness had chosen Elizabeth for a holocaust to His glory, to console Him for the outrages received from His ungrateful children, one day showed her the horrible sacrileges committed in His Church. She was so cruelly affected at the sight that she felt as if she should die of grief.

Another time He revealed to her and placed before her eyes the sins of His own Ministers and of the public Magistrates. Elizabeth was so much surprised that she was filled with profound indignation, and opened her lips to cry out for justice against these unknown delinquents; but Our Lord prevented her, and said in a tone of love and tenderness: "Ah! My daughter, cry for mercy, not for justice. I wish not the death of the sinner, but that he should be converted and live." Whilst saying these ineffable words He directed upon her from His Heart a ray of pure and living light; then he added: "May this ray of light serve you to protect men against the anger of Divine Justice."

But Our Lord showed Himself terrible against the members of those abominable secret societies, who, taking the part of hell against the Church of God, pretend to overthrow all authority, human and divine.

He allowed her to move Him only in favour of two young men who, repenting of their crime, had come with tears to ask the aid of her prayers, the application of the Blood of Jesus Christ, and the all-powerful protection of the Mother of God.

If she were ready to give a thousand lives for the salvation of souls in general, it is easy to comprehend the ardour and industry of her zeal for those who were dear to her. She never ceased to watch over all the members of her own family, brothers, sisters, and all other relatives, so as to warn them against dangers, and draw them away from occasions of sin. The care which she took to inspire her daughters with sentiments of virtue was beyond all praise. But her zeal on account of her husband was perhaps yet more heroic. Notwithstanding all her wrongs, she showed herself as attentive and submissive to him as if he had surrounded her with marks of his kindness.

Night and day she reminded him of the price of his soul, and invited him to repent; and although her advice was met by only disdain and rebuffs, she renewed it with unalterable patience and sweetness.

CHAPTER XIX

Elizabeth esteems herself as the greatest sinner in the world.—She gives herself up to the lowest and meanest occupations.—Her exercises to obtain holy humility.—Her repugnance to exposing the lights which possessed her.—Terms of deep disdain in which she addressed herself.—Her happiness when she is despised or injured.—Praises were a punishment to her.—Example of her humility in the apparition of His Holiness Pius VI.

HUMILITY is the basis of all virtues; wheresoever the edifice of heroic perfection is raised, it is certain that humility, in a sublime degree, will be found. It is also a necessary foundation upon which Our Lord may dispose of His bounties and extraordinary favours. The choicest graces, without humility, are more dangerous than useful; instead of transforming men into Angels, they pervert the Angels themselves, and transform them into devils.

Before crowning a soul with splendour and glory, Our Lord begins by ensuring for it a solid foundation against the intoxication of self-love, to prevent its falling into the abyss of pride. God having placed no limits to the extent of His munificence with regard to Elizabeth, had enriched her with a boundless humility.

But this virtue, secret in its nature, could only be appreciated by those who were about her, intimately and familiarly; so that we will quote again the words of Signora Josephine Mora, the daughter of the Venerable Mother, and her intimate and faithful companion during more than twenty-five years: "The entire course of the heroic life of my venerable mother was, as it were, nothing but one continual act of disparagement of herself. She esteemed herself so little that she regarded herself as the most perverse and criminal creature on the face of the earth. She was astonished that Our Lord would accept her sufferings and austerities for the advantage of her neighbour and the Church. According to her, all her penances would not have sufficed to expiate her abominable sins. She went to confession nearly every day, and always shedding a torrent of tears. She said that her heart was pierced by her ingratitude to God, and her negligence in corresponding with so many graces received. She believed herself worthy of a thousand hells, and to be trampled under the feet of demons for all eternity.

"In the house she applied herself to the lowest and most menial offices, making herself the servant of the servants themselves. She went into the kitchen to help the cook, she carried in the wood and charcoal, she washed the dishes, she swept, not only the rooms, but even the poultry-house and the other offices. There was no filth so repulsive that she would not undertake to clean it, even among the poor, either in the hospital or in their attics, where she willingly went to visit them. Humility was so dear to her that she practised without trouble its most heroic acts; knowing that this virtue is singularly pleasing to God, she loved it with a holy passion. In order that she might never lose sight of her poverty, and to preserve this low esteem of herself, she never ceased to ask this grace from God by continual prayer, incessant mortifications, and perpetual meditation on her own nothingness.

"By this means she showed herself invincible in presence of the attacks which she had to bear on the part of her own family. Her relations turned her into ridicule, and overwhelmed her with sneers and reproaches. Her simple manner of dressing and the humility of her actions drew upon her cruel mortifications. Her love of humility had even made her embrace some habits repugnant to nature; but her Confessor having forbidden her to continue them, she promptly obeyed, preferring obedience to all the rest. She would willingly have drawn upon herself the contempt of every one; her desire carried her so far as to sacrifice to God even her intelligence, and to wish to appear as an idiot or a fool in the eyes of men.

"Judging herself unworthy to live with reasonable creatures, she was even content at seeing herself disdained by her husband; she cherished solitude and everything that enabled her to contemplate her baseness. Obedience alone had the power to rescue her from this voluntary isolation, and induce her to help her neighbour by her counsels. And she never ceased even then to humble herself, to exaggerate her ignorance and her sins, saying that she was not worthy to raise her head in the midst of hell, and that, placed among the devils, she would yet have to blush for her perversity. She said this in words so ardent, and with so profound a feeling of conviction, that she threw all who heard her into a state of the greatest astonishment. As to myself, I was simply enraptured at seeing her so holy, so virtuous, so full of light and knowledge, and at the same time so submissive to those who held towards her the place of God by their rank or dignity.

"From the abundance of the heart the tongue speaks. A humility so profound inspired my venerable mother with expressions so full of contempt of herself, that they could only be justified by the example of many Saints whom she perfectly imitated. She would call herself filth, nothing, a creature worse than a beast, guilty of perjury to God Himself and worthy by her sins to be despised by the whole human race. It gratified her to say that she was an ignoramus, without any knowledge or talents; a useless woman, and good for nothing, etc.

"The most harmonious sound to the ears of a vain and proud person is that of his own praises; but to my humble mother, that of blame and reproach was most agreeable. She was not spared even in public by the members of the family, and she lived before witnesses, ill-treated, injured, turned into ridicule, even by the servants, whom the example of our relations had rendered bold and forward. We have heard her spoken of as imbecile, mad, and even as a sorceress and a woman possessed by the devil. But all these insults only gave greater splendour to the virtue of our heroic mother, and caused her profound humility to shine forth more brightly.

"Then her countenance might be seen to change, and appeared suffused with a celestial joy. She then experienced transports which she could scarcely contain, and which induced her to thank and overwhelm with kindness those who had so well entered into her views. Nevertheless, one thing grieved her when these odious scenes had taken place in public: this was that the witnesses of her patience and her sweetness became softened, and often loud in her praises. Demonstrations such as these mingled the bitterness of wormwood with the sweetness of her chalice, and troubled her composure.

"Many persons who appreciated her heroic virtue could not be prevented from giving her marks of their esteem and admiration. These just judges of our holy mother inflicted upon her, without knowing it, a cruel martyrdom. We heard her, at these times, repeating in a low voice: 'Not to us, O Lord! not to us, but to Thy adorable Name be the glory,' and at the same time she took refuge in the abyss of her nothingness as in a sure and inviolable asylum. She also tried by clever and pleasant words to turn the thoughts of those who praised her to some other subject, and so to change the conversation. These almost incredible sentiments of humility were preserved by our pious mother until the last hour of her life, although Our Lord, Who is pleased to exalt the humble, showered upon her the most extraordinary graces and gifts, and made her the treasurer of His most precious favours.

"The confidence which people showed in her at first appeared strange to her; but at length she consoled herself by thinking that they were weak and subject to error. But she was most puzzled and disturbed by seeing that the Saints themselves attached value to her mediation and prayers.

"On the 17th of June, 1814, my holy mother had just come from church, and, having returned home, she was occupied with household affairs, when her spirit was suddenly ravished in God. In this condition, which lasted for about three hours, she received sublime communications and signal graces. At the end, the Holy Pontiff, Pius VI, appeared to her, and told her to pray for him, because He was detained in Purgatory for negligences committed in the exercise of the Sovereign Pontificate. My venerable mother, astonished to the last degree at seeing such an illustrious personage claim the aid of her poor prayers, exclaimed: 'What do you expect from me, soul blessed by God? Do you not know that I am the vilest and most miserable creature of all who inhabit the earth? Go and find those who are the Spouses of Jesus Christ, and they will obtain for you the grace which you desire.' Then, seized with the thought of her poverty and want of virtue, she began to weep bitterly.

"But the holy Pontiff, far from being moved by these humble representations, only renewed his request, and begged for her mediation in a more pressing manner. The venerable mother, moved with compassion for the sufferings of so August a personage, asked him what he wished her to do to deliver him from the torments of Purgatory. The holy soul replied: 'Go and find your spiritual Father; obedience will teach you what you should do to open for me the gates of the Blessed. On my side, I promise you that I will never desert you, but that I will be a powerful protector to you in heaven.' After saying these words, he disappeared.

"Early in the morning of the following day, my virtuous mother went to her Confessor, related to him all that had passed, and asked him what she should do. The Rev. Father Ferdinand ordered her to go five times to visit the tomb of S. Pius V. and the holy martyrs who repose in the Church of S. Pudentiana. The servant of God obeyed without delay. Arrived at the tomb of His Holiness S. Pius V., she became recollected in prayer. Soon she was ravished in spirit, and saw that God, in His sovereign goodness, deigned to accept her prayer, and comply with her request.

"A result so favourable inspired her with a respectful boldness, and she began to solicit the deliverance of the eminent Pontiff. Our Lord replied to her: 'I leave the deliverance of this soul to your own choice.' Surprised beyond expression by such a remarkable favour, she knew not at first what to reply; then she said: 'O my God, Goodness Infinite, let me go and submit to obedience the favour which Thou doest me, and allow the day to be appointed by my spiritual Father.' This act of submission very much pleased Our Lord, and he agreed that the day should be named by her Confessor.

"Early on the following morning, she went to her spiritual

Father, and explained to him all that has been related. Her Confessor said: 'I command you to beg of Our Lord that this soul should not pass this day in Purgatory.' He repeated the same command in these terms: 'Take care that this soul does not pass another night in Purgatory. Say to Our Lord that this is the obedience which is imposed on you, and conjure Him to hear you.'

"The servant of God left her Confessor, threw herself on her knees, and whilst shedding a torrent of tears, she prayed in this manner: 'Most amiable Jesus, You have heard the order imposed upon me by Your worthy Minister, grant me the favour to be able to obey it.' Our Lord revealed to her that she was heard, and that at the hour of Vespers this soul would enter the sojourn of eternal bliss. At the hour of Vespers, she understood that the Divine promise was accomplished, and began to praise, bless, and return thanks to God for all His mercies.

"On the morning of the next day, after Holy Communion, she saw the August Pontiff before the throne of Infinite Majesty. Then turning towards him, she began to beg of him to remember her and the Church, in the following terms: 'O holy and venerated Pontiff, pray for the Church, and pray especially for the city of Rome. I unite my poor prayers to the fervour of yours. God shows Himself to us, filled with a just anger, on account of the monstrous sins which outrage Him. He is especially angry with our city of Rome, on account of its ingratitude. The chastisement which He has destined for us is already prepared. After chastisements of all sorts, He will deprive us of the privilege of possessing the Apostolic See. Oh! unhappy city! to what a distance from thee will the Holy See be taken, without the prayers of this just and holy Pontiff! Rejoice, O city of Rome, because owing to him the Apostolic See will not be ravished from thee! However, thou wilt not escape from the scourges which are the just punishment of thy violation of the Divine Commandments.' Then the holy Pontiff spoke. He returned great thanks to my venerable mother for having abridged his sufferings, promised to aid her with all his influence with God during the remainder of her life, and assured her that her continual prayer had greatly contributed to preserve Rome from the misfortunes that threatened it."

Here ends the narrative of Mother Mary Josephine. The beautiful soul of her venerable mother is depicted in this single circumstance of her life. Here is shown her ardent zeal for her neighbour and the Church, and especially her remarkable humility, which gave an inestimable value to all her actions, and fills us with wonder at the power of God, Who takes His delight among the lowly and humble of heart.

CHAPTER XX

The Venerable Mother, filled with virtue, approaches her end.—Wonderful visions which announce her deliverance, and make her long for Heaven.—Her illness declares itself at the end of 1824.—Its strange and supernatural character.—She is suddenly cured, and when it was believed that she was restored to perfect health, she foretold her imminent death.—Our Lord leaves her the choice of life or death; she prefers death.—She prepares herself for Eternity.—She suddenly expires whilst speaking to, and blessing, her children.— Her burial.

ELIZABETH had arrived at that supreme degree of sanctity to which Our Lord had called her. She had fulfilled her glorious task, she had now only to receive her just reward. Our Lord forewarned her that the day of her deliverance was approaching, and that the trials and sorrows of her pilgrimage were about to end.

One day, heaven was suddenly opened before her eyes; she saw a road, clear and resplendent as crystal, which led her to a marvellous city, whose inhabitants seemed to live in the enjoyment of all kinds of delights. Unable to turn away her eyes, she kept them for a long time fixed on this ravishing place. She felt burning desires born and multiplied in the depths of her heart, whose ardour she knew not how to contain. She languished in a delicious sorrow and the tenderest love.

God Himself unveiled His face before her, and showed to His beloved as much as a terrestrial creature can see during this mortal life. This contemplation, face to face with the God of love, penetrated her with an unknown fire, and intoxicated her with inexpressible happiness. The Heavenly Father showed her a splendid crown, whose brilliancy would have eclipsed a thousand suns, and many glorious palms; He said to her: "These are what My Son has merited for you; endeavour to ensure their possession to yourself."

From that time Elizabeth could only support life by the force of courage, and by her submission to the Will of God. Her mind and her heart already dwelt in heaven, and it was only at the price of a most painful effort that she could attend to domestic affairs. The following account was given by her to her spiritual Father regarding the beatific vision of which we have spoken:

"If the joy which my poor heart has experienced during this passing union is so great, what then will be that of my spirit when, disengaged from the bonds of this miserable mortality, it will be free to throw itself into the bosom of God? This desire has made me forget every other pleasure. Nothing can please me, however beautiful, nothing comforts me, nothing rejoices me; on the contrary, everything tires and disgusts me, no matter how agreeable it may be. There is only one thought which moves me, that is, that the happy time approaches when I shall be at full liberty to love my God. This thought alone consoles me and rejoices my heart. Be it understood that in everything I rely only on the merits of Jesus Christ, my amiable Lord; in Him alone rest all my hopes."

Our Lord now took pleasure in inflaming these burning desires, and in order to stir up the fire which consumed His beloved He often whispered in the ear of her soul: "Come, then, to My Father." At length the time arrived when a mysterious illness, which was at first believed to be a dropsy without danger, showed itself, and began to undermine the body which enchained this beautiful soul to a world which was not worthy of her. The life of the innocent Elizabeth had been wholly angelic; her death, as we might say, was a celestial one. In order that we may not conceal any circumstance from the pious curiosity of our readers, we will give the account of Mother Mary Josephine, in whose arms she gave up her last sigh. She makes us, as it were, ocular witnesses of this precious death:

"The illness which deprived us of our holy mother declared itself at the end of December, 1824. An interior fire consumed her, but according to the opinion of the physician it was not accompanied with fever. Although her legs were swollen, the courageous invalid would not neglect her ordinary duties, either by day or by night. Notwithstanding her infirmities, she heard Holy Mass every morning in her chapel, received Holy Communion, and there spent nearly all the day, and a great part of the night. Her limbs had become very feeble, but the vigour of her mind supplied the weakness of her body.

"She endured this suffering—now become chronic, but not of a dangerous character—during the whole of the month of January, 1825. In the beginning of February the malady suddenly ceased, and our venerable mother became quite well, and seemed to be growing young again. One day she laughingly said to us: 'See, my children, I begin to look younger than you.' The happiness which we experienced on seeing our mother in such flourishing health was inexpressible. But she said to us: 'My children, do not deceive yourselves by the false appearance of my health. I have only a few days to live, and, as I have often told you, my end will come when it is least expected.'

"All that occurred during that short illness was worthy of admiration. The sentiments which she expressed were heavenly. The gift of ecstasy remained with her until the last moment; she often seemed deprived of feeling. We knew that she lived only by the extraordinary redness of her countenance: a joyousness and a kind of brilliancy which I cannot describe shone from her eyes. Her breathing alone was slow and deep. The physician, astonished, said that this illness was not natural, and every one else was of the same opinion. At length, reviving from her ecstasy, she burst forth in burning expressions of love for God. At any moment she broke off the conversation by ejaculatory prayers such as: 'Oh! how sweet it is to love God!' But that which she most frequently repeated was as follows: 'O my soul! free thyself from this veil of mortality, and fly to heaven, into the arms of thy God.' She said these words and others of the same kind with so much tenderness, and so earnestly, that those who were present were moved to tears.

"Finally, on the 5th February, which fell on a Saturday, Father Ferdinand, her Confessor, came himself to celebrate Holy Mass in the Chapel. My pious mother was present at it, received Holy Communion, and, being placed upon her bed, she entered into an ecstasy which lasted the whole morning. During all this time she sent up sighs to heaven, but without speaking. She seemed to have become estranged from everything terrestrial and sensible, and as if she could no longer be moved except by heavenly things. We had all the trouble in the world to make her take some nourishment after mid-day.

"At a late hour in the evening her Confessor returned, and she had a long conversation with him; after this was ended, without coming out of her recollected state, she began, with great liberty of spirit, to occupy herself with household affairs, and to put all in order for her approaching departure.

"At seven o'clock in the evening she called me, and said: 'Listen, now that we are alone I wish to tell you what you must do after my death.' At these words I at once refused to listen, but she stopped me, and obliged me to pay attention. She then added: 'All my writings, which I have composed through obedience, and in virtue of a formal command, you will send to my Confessor. I should have wished to burn them, but obedience would not permit it. You will send him also this little bag, which contains my instruments of penance. Take yourself the little money which remains, and say nothing of it to any one. Your sister has already had more than you have had, having received all that she required on the day of her marriage. Remain always united. I leave you for your Father and Protector, Jesus of Nazareth; I place you under the mantle of the Blessed Virgin and S. Joseph. Do not trouble yourself; remain tranquil and at peace, waiting for the hour decreed by the Almighty. I remind you of the promise you have made, that you and your sister will lay me out yourselves.'

"At these words I exclaimed: 'Oh! mamma, do not speak of such sad things. You are not in a state in which there is any danger of death. If you were, Father Ferdinand would certainly have told us. We have left ourselves in his hands, and he has formally promised to inform us when the time shall come. And, as yet, nothing has been said by him to forebode such a fearful misfortune. You are under obedience to him, and you can do nothing without his telling you beforehand.'

Chapter XX

"Mamma replied: 'What you say is true, my daughter; but the thoughts of God are different from those of men. Listen to what I have to tell you. This morning, after Holy Communion, the Blessed Virgin appeared to me amidst a multitude of angelic Spirits; she took my soul and carried it before the Throne of God. On finding myself in the presence of the Divine Majesty I was sunk in the abyss of my own nothingness. Then Our Lord, with extreme goodness, gave me the choice of continuing to live on earth or to go to love Him in heaven. For myself, I was quite confused, and did not know what to say, wishing only in all things to do His good pleasure and His adorable Will. Then, remembering that He had promised me heaven, I reminded Him of His promise. Then He assured me that within a few hours he would call me to the triumph of Eternal Glory.

"'I have not failed to say all this to my Confessor; but I remarked that his mind was obscured, and that he was far from understanding what I said to him. Our Lord has permitted this, because He is the absolute Master of my soul; He does not wish that His Minister shall retain me on earth by virtue of obedience, when He Himself calls me to heaven.'

"On hearing words so clear and precise, I believed that I should die of grief; I was beside myself; and in this suspense I remained without knowing what to do. But mamma hastened to say to me: 'My child, there is no time to lose. Have the goodness to pour out some water, so that I may wash my hands and face; give me my linen chemise, as well as my jacket and collar. I must change and get myself ready. By doing so, there will remain very little for you to do.' She continued to make some recommendations to me, and to give me advice. At that moment one of her nephews, the son of her brother, arrived, who had come expressly to hear how she was. He asked her how she was; mamma replied, with perfect tranquillity: 'I am on the point of leaving you.' It was then eight o'clock. My eldest sister, who had come to help me, said: 'Since Philip is here, we can place a lower bench at the foot of the bed; mamma's feet will not be so high upon the cushions, and she will sleep better to-night.' She said this, because the swelling of her legs had reappeared, and our beloved invalid breathed with difficulty. Mamma hearing her, smiled, and said: 'You are giving yourself useless trouble.' My sister replied: 'Leave us alone, mamma, and you will see how comfortable you will be.' 'Very well,' she replied; 'do as you please.' Whilst her bed was being arranged, mamma rested upon my right arm. My sister arranged the pillows; my cousin Philip and the servant waited for the moment when they could change the bench. Then my mother, without being worse, without showing the slightest emotion, said to my sister: 'Leave the pillows there, and come and place yourself before me.' My sister said: 'Mamma, I cannot do so; if I go to you, everything will fall to the floor.' 'No matter,' mamma replied, 'leave everything to fall, and come here.' Then seeing that her daughter did not obey her, she said: 'Very well; let Victoria hold the pillows, and do you come here before me.' This time my sister obeyed. She came and placed herself by my side; my cousin was opposite the bed. When mamma saw her daughters before her, she looked at them attentively, raised her eyes, which shone like two stars, to heaven, laid herself down upon the bed, as if she meant to sleep, and resting her head upon my neck, she expired!

"As she had given no sign of death, we believed that she had fallen into an ecstasy, and we sent for her Confessor, so that he might call her back by the virtue of obedience. Father Ferdinand came indeed, but he saw that mamma was really dead. He then acknowledged to us that in the morning he had not understood anything of what she had said, and he had remained quite confused by it. Then he said: 'Our Lord has been pleased to guide this soul Himself, without human aid, through the three illnesses, or rather through the three trials which He has made of her fidelity and love. You may rejoice, you who are her daughters; you have a powerful advocate in heaven. I hope that she will also interest herself for me, who have directed her during these latter years, during which she has shown herself so exemplary and obedient.'

Chapter XX

"When my pious mother expired so sweetly in Our Lord, she was aged forty-nine years, two months, and fifteen days. She was tall, and her figure well proportioned. Her complexion was white and pure as a lily, and her cheeks the colour of a rose. Her expression was bright, but of an angelic modesty. Her nose was well shaped, and her whole profile beautiful. Her mouth and lips harmonised with the beauty of her countenance. Her whole appearance breathed ardour and vivacity; but her deportment was so grave and dignified, that she inspired devotion and respect in all who saw her..."

When her daughters were convinced that their mother was really dead, they desired to fulfil religiously her last wishes. She was dressed in the tunic of the Tertiaries of the Order of the Blessed Trinity: a carpet was spread upon the floor of the domestic chapel, and there the mortal remains of the servant of God were respectfully deposited.

The news of this unexpected death had scarcely become known, when the room was filled with relatives, neighbours, and friends; all speaking of the departed as of a real Saint. The Priest who usually said Mass in her domestic chapel came to celebrate It on the day following her glorious decease, which was a Sunday. After having finished the Holy Sacrifice, he said before all present: "From the time when I first had the honour to celebrate the Holy Sacrifice in this chapel, and I had the opportunity of conversing for a short time with this servant of God, my whole life was changed, and I began to comprehend what was meant by perfection."

Those who came in crowds to visit the venerable deceased loudly praised God for the graces granted to His faithful servant. No one thought of praying for her soul. Her daughters themselves could not finish a De Profundis. "We had scarcely begun," said Mother Mary Josephine, "when we hastened to the Gloria Patri; it seemed to ns that we heard the angels singing the Alleluia and the versicle, 'Open, ye eternal gates,' etc."

Madame Mary Josephine requested that the body should remain until the Monday: it exhaled an agreeable odour. The authorities acceded to her request. The pious daughter passed nearly the whole of these two days and two nights at the feet of her holy mother, being unable to stop praying, or contemplating her beautiful features. Death had respected the graces which adorned this body so perfectly purified by penance and the practice of every virtue; every one loved to see her; instead of inspiring horror, she attracted and captivated all eyes.

On the Monday evening, the funeral cortège went from the Rue Rasella to the Church of S. Charles dei Quattre Fontane. The Franciscan Monks of Ara-Cœli accompanied it with torches, and a great number of persons followed them. On Tuesday, the Feast of S. John of Matha (one of the Founders of the Trinitarian Order) was celebrated in the Church of S. Charles. On account of this great solemnity, the Monks could not perform a funeral service; and the burial of the Venerable Mother was put off until the next day, Wednesday, the 9th of February. The holy remains were only placed in the funeral vault on the evening of that day, amid the prayers and tears of the Fathers and Brothers of this pious and austere Community, and a multitude of others. Although the body was exposed to the air during five days, it was preserved from all corruption, and appeared like that of a person asleep. Many persons, struck by so many wonderful circumstances, would not leave the church either day or night, so long as the holy departed was exposed there.

These precious relics were deposited in the most honourable place in the funeral vault, and Father Ferdinand placed the following inscription over the modest monument which contained them:

D. O. M.
HERE REPOSES THE BODY OF
MARY ELIZABETH CANORI MORA;
WHOSE SOUL,
ADORNED BY HEROIC CHARITY
AND ENRICHED WITH

Chapter XX

SINGULAR DIVINE GIFTS,
TOOK ITS FLIGHT TO HEAVEN
ON THE 5TH OF FEBRUARY, 1825.

CHAPTER XXI

Apparitions and miracles which took place after the glorious death of the servant of God.—She recommends her daughters to her sister, Signora Maria Canori.—She gives advice to various persons.—The sick were instantaneously cured by touching her holy remains, and others by invoking her after her burial.—Various apparitions in the Monastery of the Philippine Nuns dei Monti.—Striking conversion of Christopher Mora, the husband of the Venerable Mother.

THE ILLUSTRIOUS servant of God had scarcely closed her eyes, when Our Lord hastened to glorify her upon earth by apparitions and marvellous cures. He had waited, it would seem, to reveal to men the concealed treasure of her merits, so as to show that they had in her a powerful intercessor at the Throne of His Mercy.

At the moment when she left this world with so much serenity and sweetness, her sister, Mary Canori, was kneeling at the foot of her bed, recollectedly making her evening devotions, and without having any idea of what was taking place. Suddenly Elizabeth appeared to her as vividly as if she were still living, and said to her: "I am going to the Heavenly country. I recommend you to take care of my daughters until they are established."

Mary Canori was not in the habit of seeing supernatural apparitions. This one threw her into a state of profound astonishment. Then recovering herself, she reflected that her pious sister had not appeared on that day to be in danger of death; and, at length, she forced herself to believe that her eyes had deceived her, and she slept without thinking any more of what had occurred. However, as soon as the morning of the following day arrived, she went to her sister's house, in order to explain to herself the occurrence of the previous evening, and she then learnt that her venerable sister had indeed breathed her last sigh at the time of the apparition, and that the vision had really taken place.

At the same time that the holy departed appeared to her sister, she was also seen by a young girl named Mary Bianchi, who was sick and sitting on her bed. She was waiting for her mother to bring her a slight supper before going to bed, when suddenly the Venerable Mother appeared before her, resplendent with glory, and said to her: "Mary, I am going to heaven, do not forget to confess that sin which you had forgotten." When she had said those words she disappeared.

The sick girl uttered a cry, called her mother, and said to her: "Look! what is the time?" She then added, with great excitement: "Ah! mamma, Mother Elizabeth has just gone to heaven."

Her mother replied: "My child, you are dreaming with your eyes open."

"That is impossible," said the daughter. "It is strange if this be not true! But to-morrow we will verify the time." Then suddenly bursting into tears, she said: "Ah! mamma, as a proof of the truth, she has revealed to me a sin which I had forgotten to mention in confession, and she ordered me to confess it. She also told me that I also shall lead a holy life, and that I shall die a holy death. See, then, if I am deceived, or if I am dreaming."

The next morning the mother heard of the death of the Venerable Mother, and she saw that her daughter had told the truth.

She appeared also to many persons in the town of Marino, where she had received, during her lifetime, great marks of esteem and kindness. She appeared on the evening of her death to one of her friends, and said to her: "If you desire to come where I am going you must walk in the thorny path of which I have often spoken to you, and you must put in practice the advice which I have so often given you during my lifetime. Be assured that I shall never forget any member of your family. Tell them all that they may with confidence rely upon me." After these words, so consoling to this family, she disappeared. There were many wonderful cures through her intercession, and some were instantaneous.

A woman had suffered for a long time from a tumour, and all medical skill had failed to cure it. The evil was even increasing, and had become a cancer. Having heard that the body of the Venerable Mother was exposed in the little Church of S. Charles dei Quattre Fontane, she went there. On arriving she knelt down at the feet of the deceased, prayed, and touched the coffin. Her cure was instantaneous; this happy woman returned home as well as if she had never had any ailment.

Another woman was afflicted with a tumour which presented alarming symptoms. She approached the coffin with a lively confidence, touched the clothes which covered the venerable body, and felt herself immediately cured of her disease.

Signora Maria Angela di Sanctis, of the town of Marino, an old friend of the Venerable Mother, had a little daughter, Celestine de Sanctis, who was attacked, at the age of two years, with a putrid fever. Her illness made such rapid progress that the physicians despaired of her life. Her mother, full of confidence in the sanctity of the venerable deceased, placed a thread of her veil in the water which she gave to the sick child to drink. The child had scarcely taken the salutary liquid when she felt better; she got up as if from a profound sleep, seated herself upon her bed, voluntarily took her food, which she had refused during three days, and began to amuse herself; in a few days she was quite cured. At the present time Mother Celestine de Sanctis is a Nun in the Monastery of Marino, and enjoys perfect health.

The deposition of Signor Matteo di Sanctis, the brother of Signora Maria Angela di Sanctis, of whom we have spoken, is full of a pious enthusiasm:

"I can-testify," he said, "in perfect truth, that from the age of twenty-three years" (he is now sixty-five) "I have had very delicate health, in consequence of convulsive fits and frequent attacks of asthma. But I have always had recourse to the servant of God, and I attribute to her intercession the successive cures which I have obtained, although they have never been instantaneous, and also the prolongation of my life. I have never ceased, and I will never cease, to inculcate in my family devotion to this servant of God. A few months before her death she said to me, when I was leaving the chapel: 'I have only a short time to live; but I shall always remember you, and also your family.' "

A young English lady became a prey to consumption, and was

already in an advanced stage of this disease. Hoping to obtain some benefit she had tried various changes of air in different places in the neighbourhood of Rome. But all these changes had no result, and death was rapidly advancing. To heighten the misfortune, the sick girl was a Protestant, and her soul was in danger as well as her body.

Many persons, distinguished by their rank and knowledge, made various efforts to induce her to open her eyes and to enter the bosom of the true Church; but she politely repulsed these charitable invitations, and openly declared that she would die in the religion in which she was born. The Rev. Father John, General of the Trinitarian Order, passing through the country, by a special disposition of Divine Providence, heard of the danger of this young lady and her obstinacy in heresy. He immediately decided to go and pay her a visit; he said not one word to her on the subject of religion, but he offered her the portrait of the Venerable Mother. The young lady gratefully received it, looked at it attentively, and then became recollected, as if listening to an interior voice. She soon after uttered the following words: "I desire to abjure heresy, and to receive the Sacraments of the Catholic Church." Her attendants were astounded, and looked at each other as if they could not be sure that they had understood her. But the young girl repeated her request so distinctly that every shadow of doubt vanished.

To this first grace Our Lord vouchsafed to add another, which served as its complement. He suspended the progress of her illness, and gave her sufficient leisure for instruction, and to prepare herself to receive the Sacraments. When she was asked how such an unexpected change had been accomplished in her, she replied: "Whilst I was looking at the picture of the servant of God, I felt myself completely transformed interiorly. A vehement desire to die in the Faith of the Catholic Church took possession of me, and I could no longer resist so palpable an inspiration."

When she had fulfilled all her duties as a child of Holy Church, and was fully prepared for her departure into eternity, she peacefully slept in Our Lord, holding a crucifix to her heart, on which she fixed her last look.

During the month of January, 1853, a young woman was attacked by an inflammatory fever, which became complicated, and at length took a nervous character. Full of piety, she resigned herself to the Will of God, and prepared herself for death, which her physicians believed to be imminent. One of her uncles came to see her, and brought out to sort at a table, in her presence, a number of papers. The sick girl, while looking at them, fixed her attention upon a portrait. She said to her uncle: "You have a Saint among your papers—give it to me."

Her uncle replied: "I do not know who that Saint is;" and he gave it to her.

The pious girl placed the picture under her pillow, and without knowing the Venerable Mother, she recommended herself to her intercession. Her prayer was promptly heard. On the next day the physicians, when visiting her, found her free from fever. They could not help saying to her, in their surprise: "You have been the subject of a miracle." Two days later the pious girl left her bed, and found herself so well that she could undertake, without delay, her ordinary occupations.

Some time after an aunt of this pious girl was attacked by the same illness. The girl hastened to find the precious picture which had cured her, and gave it to her aunt. This time the cure was not delayed; it was instantaneous.

The last cure known to have taken place occurred in the month of March, 1867, the person being Signora Casilda Jacobelli, of the Parish of Our Lady dei Monti, in Rome. This lady, being near her confinement, became swollen in all her limbs, and that in such a manner that it was impossible for her to put on her shoes. Even after having her legs firmly bandaged she could scarcely walk a few steps in her own room. Her family hoped that her confinement would relieve her, and remove a danger which became every day more serious. She was safely delivered of a child, but the swelling made such frightful progress in a few days that it was thought necessary to administer the last Sacraments to her.

A person named Louis Alessi learnt what was passing in the house of the Jacobellis. Full of confidence in the intercession of the servant of God, he gave her picture and a small piece of her dress to Adelaide Feroci, and begged her to take them to the sick woman. The attendants wished to give a thread of this dress in a drink to Signora Casilda, but she was reduced to so sad a state that no one could succeed in giving it to her. The Vicar of Our Lady dei Monti, who was present, attempted to give it to her, but he was not more successful than the others. Then he placed the picture and the small piece of stuff under the pillow of the dying woman, told the attendants to have confidence in God, and all together recited some prayers in honour of the Blessed Trinity.

From that moment the condition of the sick woman was sensibly ameliorated. The next day she was able to take the drink prepared on the previous evening; the swelling gradually disappeared, and with it all symptoms of illness.

The greatest and most illustrious personages have had recourse to the powerful intercession of the Venerable Mother. Cardinal Benoit Barberini, a member of the princely family of that name, was attacked by a malady which the physicians declared incurable. The Rev. Father Ferdinand of S. Louis, who had been the Confessor of the servant of God, went to visit him, gave him her portrait, and persuaded him to invoke her with confidence. The august Prelate piously received the precious picture, and with all his heart recommended himself to the intercession of the holy woman with God.

So noble an example of faith and simplicity deserved a signal recompense. The pious Cardinal was cured; and in order to declare publicly to whom he owed his life, he went to the Church of S. Charles to make his thanksgiving at the tomb of the venerable deceased. He also displayed the most sincere gratitude to the pious monk who had suggested to him so powerful a remedy.

We have said that Mother Mary Josephine Mora became a Religious in the Monastery of the Oblates of S. Philip Neri, in the

Quarter dei Monti. It was impossible that the presence of a daughter so tenderly loved by her mother should not have drawn down signal favours upon this house. Indeed, circumstances of the highest interest took place in this Convent. The Venerable Mother appeared on several occasions. One day she presented herself, radiant with glory, to Sister Benedetta Coppini. She, being harassed by an excessive fear of the judgments of God, implored her to obtain for her the grace of final perseverance. The servant of God replied: "Yes, you will be saved; but on condition that you correct a certain fault," which she mentioned. This took place in 1837.

In 1846 she appeared to Sister Teresa Ilari, and said to her: "In a short time a great misfortune will happen to you; prepare yourself for it." This prediction was verified only too soon. A few days after this warning from Heaven, Sister Teresa had the misfortune to hear of the assassination of her only brother. This good man having come upon two persons engaged in a serious quarrel, and about to bring the contest to a fatal issue, hastened to separate them. But one of them, intending to fire a pistol at his opponent, shot the unfortunate Ilari, and mortally wounded him.

The following fact took place on the 21st April, 1833. A young novice, named Maria Rosa Bernaschi, was taken seriously ill, and, in the opinion of the physician, there was no hope of her cure. Her Novice-Mistress, Sister Maria Angelica Maldura gave her a small piece of the veil of the Venerable Mother, and advised her to invoke her fervently. The sick Novice, instead of feeling any confidence in this recommendation, was inspired with repugnance rather than confidence in it. She said to herself: "What can this piece of a veil do for me? I do not believe in this sanctity which they are publishing everywhere. And then there are so many Saints in heaven: it is only just that I should recommend myself to them.

Where will all this end? I will say three Paters to the Blessed Trinity, and that will be enough." She said them, indeed, but against her will.

Suddenly, at an advanced hour of the night, the sick Novice saw the whole Noviciate illuminated more brilliantly than at midday, and in the midst of this brilliant light a lady habited in white, resplendent with glory, and full of a sweet and imposing majesty. The great Queen was followed by another person, a degree less glorious than the first. The second raised the curtain of the bed, and said: "Do you not know me, my daughter? I am Elizabeth. I have come to cure you. You may be assured that you will make your Religious profession. Take courage, then!" She then gave her some advice for the guidance of her soul.

The young Novice passed from a state of incredulity and defiance to an excess of joy. She had feared that she would be sent away from the Convent, even if she had recovered. This fear disappeared, and she began to make acts of thanksgiving to Our Lord, to the Blessed Virgin, to the Venerable Mother, and to all the Saints in Paradise. As soon as it was morning she hastened to relate everything to her mistress. When the physicians arrived they found her able to get up, and as it was a Feast she went to the choir to hear Mass. She afterwards went back to her bed because she felt herself still very weak; but two days after her strength was restored. She had the happiness to make her vows, and has ever since enjoyed perfect health.

But the most astonishing miracle accomplished by the Venerable Mother was the conversion of her husband, Christopher Mora. One day she made a prediction to him, which then seemed very unlikely to be fulfilled.

Signora Matilda Brambelli, now a Religious in Rome, came with her mother to visit the picture of Jesus of Nazareth. These ladies, on going away, spoke to Signor Mora, who laughingly said to them: "You come to pray! It is always Christmas night with my wife; but I allow her to keep it; and, for my own part, I say Mass whilst I am sleeping in my bed."

The Venerable Mother then joined in the conversation, and said to him: "Laugh as much as you please; but after my death you will say Mass, and what is more, you will hear confessions. You will then no longer pretend to say Mass in bed!"

Signor Mora continued in his usual habits as long as Elizabeth lived, but she was scarcely dead when he began to feel the effects of her power with God. He embraced a penitential life, and has been met, more than once, in the early morning, going with naked feet (human respect being quite set aside) through the streets of Rome, to hear Mass at the different churches.

He has often said, with tears in his eyes: "I sanctified my dear and holy wife by my bad conduct. Can I ever forgive myself?"

One day he went to see Mother Josephine, then an Oblate of S. Philip, and informed her that he desired to leave the world and embrace the Religious state in an austere and penitential Order. In fact he was invested with the Franciscan habit in 1834, in the Church of S. Dorothy, in the presence of his numerous relations. After a year's Noviciate away from Rome he made his solemn profession, and a short time after was raised to the dignity of the Priesthood. Being well educated, he became both Confessor and Professor, as Elizabeth had foretold. Business sometimes called him to Rome, and his happiness then was to say Mass in his daughter's Convent and give her Holy Communion with his own hand.

He spent eleven years in Religion, and died in the little town of Sezze on the 8th September, 1845, leaving behind him a blessed memory and heroic examples of obedience, humility, patience, and all religious virtues. His penances were excessive, together with his contrition for the sins of his past life, which he felt had only been forgiven through the intercession with Our Lord of his holy and venerable wife.

EPILOGUE

FROM the life of this venerable and noble woman we can learn many lessons. First, that daily trials are the most efficacious means of sanctification; God is pleased to scatter them under the feet of His elect, so that He may be able to grant them His ineffable gifts. It is a certain law of the supernatural order that the Holy Spirit enriches a soul with His most precious favours only according to the degree of its trials.

The measure of its sufferings is that of its reward. Illumined by the Divine light which we draw from the lives of the Saints, we must not shrink from the crosses which may be laid upon us. We know of no other means by which we may transform and regenerate ourselves; if we fly from trials we withdraw ourselves from heavenly graces. Our duty is not to draw them down upon ourselves by culpable imprudence, but we must lovingly embrace them when they come, and be assured that suffering will never be wanting to us on earth.

Divine Providence disposes the events of this world in such a manner that the Cross is the portion of every one of His children. Kings are not more exempt from it than the poor and the lowly. The wealthy, the learned, men of all classes and of every condition have to drink of this cup of sorrow. Happy those who thus know how to obtain the imperishable goods of eternity. The life of Elizabeth Canori Mora will afford to all of us this important lesson.

In Rome we determined to prove by our own experience the blessings which are attached to the holy water blessed by Jesus of Nazareth; and have had the consolation to experience from it the most admirable results. We have, therefore, a great desire to see the devotion to Jesus of Nazareth take root in Europe, and take possession of the souls of men, especially in these evil days.

In this devotion is a source of incomparable grace, which has been revealed to us by the life of this servant of God. This rich treasure will no longer remain a veiled secret; it will be known to all, and each of us may have recourse to it to aid us in our wants, and especially in those of a spiritual and moral order.

The life of Elizabeth Canori Mora will be for mothers also a model and a guide to direct them in their difficulties and show them how to act.

We do not know any work in which are so clearly traced the duties of a neglected and humiliated wife, who knew how to conquer for Heaven the soul of her husband, and those of many others.

We are not placed here below in order to enjoy a little passing and terrestrial happiness; the object of our destiny is far more sublime; we are bound to aid each other in the salvation of innumerable souls.

The great law of association is dominant in modern society. It is to the union of capital that we owe all the material glories of this century.

We must apply this law in the moral order for the spiritual good of our brethren, and we shall then have the happiness of seeing wonderful conversions, and admirable returns to God. Each one of us must take for our motto to strive to be useful to our neighbour for his eternal salvation; to make it our duty and consolation to pardon him; to pray for him, and to offer him a helping hand in case of need.

Union of hearts, association of prayer, fraternity in devotion, will be a lever which will raise the world; Hell will be vanquished, the rebellious flesh will submit to the yoke of the law, and grace will reign supreme in all hearts.

The Saints of our era authoritatively teach us this fundamental truth of the necessity of union to secure the triumph of the Church, which is the object of all our hopes. Prostrate at the foot of the Altar, we have often asked of God, with burning tears, to reveal to us the secret of the regeneration of souls. Then inquiring into the lives of the illustrious servants of God, especially of our time, we have sought the law by which they have become such centres of good, and a principle of salvation to so large a number of souls. It is easy to discover the mystery of their power with God; they have consented to suffer in favour of those whom they wish to bring back into the paths of virtue and piety; and their sufferings in union with Jesus and Mary have become a source of innumerable graces.

If we only knew how to unite ourselves in a holy league for the purpose of helping each other, we should have discovered the great lever of the moral and supernatural world. It is our profound conviction that God, in His mercy, will send us holy souls enlightened with His grace, who will realise for the spiritual welfare of souls what we see accomplished by the association of capital in the material and social world. Our age is sick unto death: the world is more than ever corrupt: no observing person can deny it; and nevertheless it seems indisputably true that there is also a work of regeneration in souls going on which gives the fairest hopes.

We are on the borders of an abyss; people and nations are passing through a formidable crisis; but God is preparing for us amid all these evils a remedy for the transformation of men. We await with confidence great spiritual benefits in the future.

It is true that men must submit to the crucible of suffering, but it is by these crosses that their regeneration will be accomplished, and thus the Church will possess great Saints, whose advent in the coming time has been already predicted, and whose mission will be to save our Sodom and avert the just anger of Divine Justice.

APPENDIX.

The text of the Decrees of the Sacred Congregation of Rites has already been published: the first is on the Introduction of the Cause: that is to say, the Permission to introduce it, signed by His Holiness, by virtue of which the servant of God has been declared Venerable; the second is of non culto: that is to say, that the faithful are not to pay any public cultus to the Venerable Mother—this is conformably to the Decrees of Urban VIII.

This Cause has already made some progress, and at the present moment the two Apostolic Processes of Reputation of

Sanctity and of heroic Virtues have been concluded.

All the expenses which have been incurred up to this time, as well as those which will be required for the continuation of this Cause, have been provided by the offerings of good Catholics in Italy and France, and sent to the Postulator of the Cause. These fervent Catholics, having become acquainted with the admirable life of Elizabeth Canori Mora, desired to augment the glory of God by the glorification of this Venerable Mother, who, having been the mother of a family, might be in our times proposed by the Church as the model of Christian mothers.

Those pious persons who may wish to aid in this Cause may send their offerings to the Vice-Postulator of the Cause, Brother Antonino Multon, Director of the Brothers of the Christian Schools, Rome, 14, Place Mastai, Rome; or to the Vicar-General of that Institute, the Rev. Romualdo Canori, nephew of the Venerable Mother, 10, Place de San Salvatore in Lauro, Rome.[1]

THE END

---

[1] See the next page for info on the history of Bl. Elizabeth's beatification subsequent to the original publication of this book in 1878.

Editor's Note on the Subsequent Beatification of Elizabeth Canori Mora

On 26 February 1874, by the decree *Non cultu*, the cause was formally introduced. The Promulgation of the decree on her heroic virtues was made on 26 February, 1928. Owing to delays on account of the Second World War as well as the Second Vatican Council, the decree on her miracle came on 6 June 1993, which had been verified by a diocesan inquiry and the Medical Board. As the conclusion of this process, on 24 April 1994, Pope John Paul II declared Elizabeth a Blessed, during the international year of the family.

www.ingramcontent.com/pod-product-compliance
Lightning Source LLC
Chambersburg PA
CBHW011130070526
44583CB00023B/2969